PREVIOUS TITLES IN THE SERIES

Edited by Robin Myers & Michael Harris

Development of the English Book Trade 1700–1899. OPP, 1981

Sale and Distribution of Books from 1700. OPP, 1982

Author-Publisher Relations in the Eighteenth and Nineteenth Centuries. OPP, 1983

Maps and Prints: Aspects of the English Booktrade. OPP, 1984

Economics of the British Booktrade 1605–1939. Chadwyck–Healey, 1985

Bibliophily. Chadwyck–Healey, 1986

Aspects of Printing from 1600. OPP, 1987

PIONEERS
IN
BIBLIOGRAPHY

Edited by
Robin Myers and Michael Harris

ST PAUL'S BIBLIOGRAPHIES
1988

© 1988 The Contributors

First published 1988 by
St Paul's Bibliographies,
West End House,
1 Step Terrace,
Winchester,
Hampshire SO22 5BW

British Library Cataloguing in Publication Data

Pioneers in bibliography: papers presented
at a seminar in book trade history, 27/28
November 1987.
1. Bibliography
I. Myers, Robin   II. Harris, Michael, *1938*
010

ISBN 0-906795-69-9

Typeset in Monophoto Garamond by
August Filmsetting, Haydock, St Helens
Printed in England by
Henry Ling, Dorchester

Contents

Preface   *page 7*

List of Contributors   *8*

List of those attending the conference   *9*

Christopher de Hamel   *Medieval Library Catalogues*   *11*

T.A. Birrell   *Anthony Wood, John Bagford and Thomas Hearne as Bibliographers*   *25*

Robin Myers   *Stationers' Company Bibliographers; the First Hundred Years: Ames to Arber*   *40*

David Hall   *The Earlier Bibliographers of Quakerism*   *58*

Ronald Browne   *W.C. Hazlitt and his 'Consolidated Bibliography'*   *73*

Julian Roberts   *The Bibliographical Society as a Band of Pioneers*   *86*

Esther Potter   *'Oxford Books on Bibliography'*   *101*

Preface

THIS EIGHTH VOLUME of papers of the annual conference on book trade history which is held under the auspices of the Department of Extra-Mural Studies of the University of London is published by St Paul's Bibliographies. The theme of pioneers in bibliography harked back to the 1985 conference on bibliophily and leads on to our forthcoming session on forgeries, frauds and false imprints, when we hope that Nicolas Barker, Michael Harris, Lotte Hellinga, Joseph Levine, Nigel Ramsay and Michael Treadwell will be among our speakers. In addition to the papers printed here we again organised workshop sessions which proved both popular and useful. We are grateful to Don McKenzie, Keith Maslen, Elizabeth Leedham-Green and Gwyn Walters for chairing the groups and for organising the reporting back to the full session. We are not including the reports themselves in this volume although each was concerned with a major area of bibliographical research. The session chaired by Keith Maslen, for example, which was admirably reported by Michael Winship centred on the issue of bibliography and the book trade. Instead, we have provided, thanks to the help of Anna Greening who took down what was said in shorthand, a summary of the discussions which took place after each of the papers. We list the principal participants, who can be identified in the list of conference members (pp. 9–10) in an appendix to each paper.

Although we have continued to use the term 'book trade' in our general title and to focus on the circumstances of the production and sale of books we have also enlarged our scope to accommodate such related areas of research as library and collecting history. 'Pioneers in Bibliography' is the first volume to contain a paper on a manuscript subject; we hope to continue to include a paper in this area, which is so often neglected by bibliographers, whenever possible. This year we celebrate a decade of these conferences which we believe and hope form a useful part of the varied activity concerned with the study of the book trades and the history of the book.

Robin Myers and Michael Harris
London
February 1988

Contributors

T.A. BIRRELL is a retired teacher of English, at present engaged in compiling a catalogue of the Old Royal Library. His publications include *The Library of John Morris* (British Library, 1976) and *English Monarchs and their Books* (British Library, 1987). He is editor of *English Studies*.

RONALD BROWNE is on the staff of the British Library and is primarily concerned with the cataloguing of English books printed between 1501 and 1800. He was for a number of years Librarian of the Jesuit College at Farm Street, London.

CHRISTOPHER DE HAMEL is a director of Sotheby's in charge of the sale of medieval illuminated manuscripts. He is author of *Glossed Books of the Bible and the Origins of the Paris Booktrade* and of *A History of Illuminated Manuscripts*.

ROBIN MYERS is Hon Archivist of the Stationers' Company in London. As well as acting as joint-editor of the conference papers she has written extensively on areas of book-trade history and has recently been engaged in editing the Stationers' Company Records (1554–1920) for a microfilm edition.

DAVID J HALL is an Under-Librarian at Cambridge University Library, responsible for general administration and for the Morison Room collections. He has written articles and reviews on varied bibliographical and Quaker themes and is at present working on the history of the Library of the Society of Friends.

ESTHER POTTER is a former librarian who is now working on the bibliographical papers of Graham Pollard. She is a contributor to *The Journal of Newspaper and Periodical History* on this subject.

JULIAN ROBERTS is Deputy Librarian and Keeper of Printed Books at the Bodleian Library. He is President of the Bibliographical Society, having also served as Hon Secretary for over 20 years. His current research is on the library of Dr John Dee (1527–1609) and he expects to publish Dee's 1583 Catalogue in 1988.

List of those attending the Conference

Audrey Adams
Librarian/Indexer/Bibliographer

Jean Archibald
Librarian

Alison Bailey
British Library

Professor John Barnard
University of Leeds

Jacqueline Beevers
British Library

Richard Burleigh
Bookseller

Andrew S. Cook
Map Archivist
India Office Records, British Library

Dr Karen Cook
Map Specialist
British Library

Angela Craft
Paper Conservator
Public Record Office

Miss Nest Davies
Historical research

Mrs Phyllis T.M. Davies
Retired Librarian

Mrs Michael Devas
Retired, sometime Librarian

Christine Ferdinand
Postgraduate Student
Wolfson College, Oxford

Dr Mirjam Foot
British Library

Andrew Gasson
Book collector

Anna Greening
Amenuensis

Philip Harris
British Library (retired)

Judith Harrison
British Library

C.M. Hartley
Librarian

John Hewish
British Library

A.W. Huish
Librarian (retired)

Arnold Hunt
Student
Trinity College, Cambridge

Helene Huret
Bibliography Department,
B. Quaritch

Yuji Kaneko
Professor of English
Chuo University, Tokyo

Vincent Kinane
Librarian
Trinity College, Dublin

David Laker
Banker

Colin Lee

Dr Elisabeth Leedham-Green
Archivist
University Library, Cambridge

PIONEERS IN BIBLIOGRAPHY

Dr Anthony Lister
Retired Lecturer

James McGhee
Research Student, Glasgow

Professor D.F. McKenzie
Reader in Textual Criticism, Oxford

Miss Margaret Macleod

Giles Mandelbrote
Postgraduate Student,
St John's College, Oxford

Keith Maslen
Lecturer
University of Otago,
Dunedin, New Zealand

John E.C. Palmer
British Library

Charles Parry
Assistant Librarian
National Library of Wales

Margaret Payne
Librarian

Michael Perkin
Librarian
University of Liverpool

Charles Rivington
Retired

Alison Shell
Postgraduate Student
St Hilda's College, Oxford

Peter Stockham
Bookseller and Book Consultant

Dr Katherine Swift
Keeper of Early Printed Books
Trinity College, Dublin

Michael L. Turner
Bodleian Library, Oxford

Keith Vaughan
Oxford Polytechnic (retired)

Gwyn Walters
Research Fellow
St David's University College, Wales

Tony Watts
Senior Lecturer
Oxford Polytechnic

Eva Weininger
Bookseller

H. Whiteside
British Library

Michael Winship
Postgraduate Student
Oxford

R.B. Woodings
Lecturer
Oxford Polytechnic

Peter Wright
Retired Lecturer

Medieval Library Catalogues

CHRISTOPHER DE HAMEL

A SYMPOSIUM on pioneer bibliographers faces a problem in confronting medieval book catalogues, the earliest substantial records of descriptive bibliography. Medieval catalogues of libraries are surprisingly common but the pioneers who compiled them are for the most part anonymous. When their names are known, our heroes are shadowy figures such as the librarian Chunradus Bozo who signed his library catalogue of 139 manuscripts at the Bavarian abbey of Wessobrun around 1240, or the monk Etienne de Simiane who listed the books of St André de Villeneuve-lez-Avignon in 1307, or John Whytefeld who drew up the catalogue of St Martin's prior in Dover in 1389, or Gilles Malet and Jean Blanchet, the 'valets de chambre' who catalogued the library of Charles V of France for him in 1373 and 1380. Quite as often we know only the names of the people under whose supervision library catalogues were compiled, administrators such as bishop Odelricus of Cremona in 984, abbot Wolfram of St Michelsberg in Bamberg (1112–23), and prior Henry of Eastry (d.1331) of Christ Church cathedral priory in Canterbury. Bare names like these represent the real pioneers of bibliography. We can only approach them through their catalogues. Such monuments exist in great numbers. Nearly 350 medieval library catalogues had been published by the time of the first list of them in 1885 and over 1750 had been recorded by 1890.[1] Very many (and perhaps the majority) of medieval monasteries kept inventories of their possessions and of their manuscripts, and in the later middle ages many universities and other colleges and even private individuals made lists of their holdings in books.

Many of the French medieval library catalogues were published either in the 19th-century catalogues of the French municipal libraries or in Léopold Delisle's *Cabinet des Manuscrits* between 1868 and 1881.[2] The German and Swiss and Austrian catalogues have been edited in vast volumes over the last 75 or so years by various editors including Paul Lehmann, Paul Ruf and Gerlinde Möser-Mersky.[3] The English library catalogues delighted the Victorian ecclesiastical antiquaries and M.R. James, and were often published in unusual topographical journals and lives of bishops; they are now being collected up and re-edited for the new Corpus of British Medieval Library Catalogues of which the first volumes are nearing completion.

Medieval catalogues of libraries are of interest to many modern readers. Historians of texts watch tantalising references to books in circulation, unattested by surviving manuscripts. A little catalogue of classical texts survives from the court of Charlemagne about 790, for instance, and includes some books, such as Lucretius and the Elder Seneca, earlier than any known manuscripts survive. If one is studying the learning of a community or a famous individual, nothing is more effective for coming to an understanding of their intellectual achievements than knowing what resources were at their disposal and what books they may have been able to read first. Manuscripts that happen to survive can only give a very partial picture of what was once there. References to texts, contemporary attributions of author, sources of exemplars or donors, names of scribes and illuminators, script, bindings, cost of books, library furniture, display and chaining of books, frequency of repairs, loans, reader admissions, and so forth, all fascinating for their own sake, can be found by browsing in library catalogues. I have to confess to finding medieval library catalogues quite irresistible. Almost anyone today visiting a house for the first time and seeing a wall full of books, can run a critical eye along the titles and learn a great deal about a person's taste and background from the books they buy and from the volumes which look read and the volumes which do not. With a good inventory, one can make just such judgements about a man who died a thousand years ago.

Two very grand such catalogues are those of Charles V of France and of his younger brother the Duc de Berry.[4] These list page after page of quite detailed descriptions of manuscripts: wonderful texts, romances, marvels, chronicles, bestiaries, a lot of astronomy and medicine, and many richly illuminated books of devotion. Here, for instance, is an Arthurian romance:

Du roy Artus de la Table ronde et de la mort du dit roy, très bien escript, et enluminé, en trois coulombez, de grant volume.

Surviving Arthurian manuscripts are often vast, almost square, volumes with the triple column layout. This in Charles V's library list in 1373 is annotated with a note that Charles V borrowed it one day and that Charles VI authorised its loan to the Queen on 20 April 1401.[5] Little facts like this, giving glimpses of how the royal family used their books, occur hundreds and hundreds of times. Often the bindings are described, especially for prayer books. Here is a graphic description of one Book of Hours kept in Charles V's study in 1380:

Ung livre dont les aiz sont de brodeure aux armes de la royne Jehanne de Bourbon, et dedens sont les Heures de Nostre Dame et unes Sept pseaulmes, à deux fermoirs d'or à façon de treffle, esmaillées de ses armes, En l'estude du Roy à Vincennes.[6]

The manuscript is not known to survive. It was bound in wooden boards embroidered with the arms of Charles's late wife Jeanne de Bourbon (1338–77) and had gilt trefoil clasps enamelled with her arms. Knowledge of such bindings must now derive almost exclusively from medieval catalogue descriptions. We have at Sotheby's the late Geoffrey Hobson's copies of these French royal inventories and his ecstatic exclamation marks on the bindings are a delight to see: bindings covered with red silk with red clasps of silver gilt; bindings of stamped red calf with 4 pewter clasps; bindings in velvet with pictures on the sides sewn with pearls and with gold clasps inlaid with the arms of France, all wrapped in damask cloth. These catalogues give information too about how the books were obtained, whether inherited or by gift or by purchase (and who from), and, if they left the library (as often happened) where they went. This anthology of texts was sent to the Duc de Berry in 1403 by his tactful 14-year-old nephew Gianmaria Visconti (1389–1412):

Un livre en latin des Epistres de Senèque, de saint Pol et d'autres, ouquel sont contenus pluseurs autres livres, escript de lettre lombarde, à deux fermoirs d'argent dorés, esmaillés aux armes du duc de Milan, qui l'envoya à Monseigneur en mars 1403.[7]

It is appropriate that this manuscript dispatched from Milan should have been in 'lettre lombarde'. Script is often described: sometimes books are 'en très bonne et grosse lettre', 'de lettre de forme', 'de lettre courant', 'de lettre boulonnoise', or sometimes 'mal escript' or 'de mauvaise lettre'. When we can match these with extant manuscripts, we can begin to understand how a medieval book-user classified available scripts and how he judged their age or quality.

Both Charles V and his brother had some tantalising antiquarian books. Two Psalters which had belonged to St Louis were kept in Charles's bed-chamber in the château at Vincennes.[8] One can note with envy the Duc de Berry's manuscript:

Un très ancien Psautier long, historié d'ouvrage romain, et au commencement de David jouant de la harpe...[9]

This book was given to the Sainte-Chapelle and survives. It is not wrong to call the illumination 'd'ouvrage romain' because the book was made in the second quarter of the 11th century in England, perhaps at Canterbury.[10] It would be fascinating to be able to trace one day the Psalter which is said to have belonged to St Thomas Becket:

Un Psautier bien ancien, historié le kalendrier et ailleurs en pluseurs lieux, qui fu de saint Thomas de Canturbiere.[11]

Identifiable books in the Duc de Berry's library list include the *Très Riches Heures* (with the sole documentary evidence that the Limbourg brothers, 'Pol et ses frères', painted this, the greatest extant medieval manuscript), the *Belles Heures*, 'lesquelles heures monseigneur a fait faire par ses ouvriers' (now in the Cloisters Museum), the *Grandes Heures*, 'de la main Jaquemart de Hodin et autres ouvriers de Monseigneur' (now in the Bibliothèque Nationale), and very many more, some of which would certainly have eclipsed even those, if they had survived.

The sort of catalogue which lists these grand manuscripts is really only an inventory – not a bibliographical tool – and it records books like any other valuable treasures in the royal palaces. The descriptions are mixed up with records of goldwork and jewels and precious enamels; they are proofs of wealth rather than guides for a reader seeking a text in a library. Detailed descriptions of bindings hint that the volumes are being checked off without even opening them. The same inventorial purpose occurs in some of the earliest known library catalogues. The list of classical texts in Charlemagne's palace has already been mentioned. Two of Charlemagne's successors, Louis the Pious in 831 and Lothair in 881, commanded monasteries to list their assets, and in response to the first edict the monks of St Riquier Abbey catalogued their library, arranged probably as it was actually stored: 176 theological books in the monastery itself ('codices librorum claustralium'), then manuscripts for the abbey school and classical texts on history and geography, and finally books in the Sacristy used for divine service including various types of Missal and choirbook together with a Gospel Book 'aureis litteris scriptus' which sounds very splendid and was doubtless extremely valuable. All this was transcribed into the chronicle of the abbey.[12] In 984 Odelricus, bishop of Cremona (973–1004), ordered an inventory of the treasury in the porch of his Cathedral, and they listed 64 books followed by 31 more which the munificent bishop himself gave, including a Gospel Book and a Benedictional written in gold.[13]. Bindings are sometimes described simply because they were so lavish. The inventory of 17 books at Staffelsee Abbey in 812 includes a Lectionary with boards ornamented with sheets of copper gilt and in a cloth cover.[14] The 10th-century catalogue of Lorsch Abbey opens with a Gospel Book embellished with golden writing and having covers of ivory.[15] The actual manuscript survives, now divided between Alba Julia in Rumania and the Vatican Library, and one of its ivory covers, which was mentioned a thousand years ago, has passed by a complicated descent to the Victoria and Albert Museum.

By no means all Carolingian manuscripts were in gold and ivory and to imply that catalogues merely record frivolous luxury would be to understate the Carolingian determination to build up rich storehouses of texts. Striking evidence of this achievement is in the library catalogue of Reichenau Abbey on Lake Constance in 821–2. The *Brevis Librorum* drawn up then lists 415 books arranged by subjects: biblical books, major patristic writers (Augustine, Jerome, Gregory, Leo, Cyprian, and so on) through to Aldhelm, Boethius and Alcuin (who had died only 18 years before), followed by canons, homilies, monastic rules, martyrologies, glossaries, and a miscellaneous group of grammatical and verse texts, including two copies of Virgil.[16] Among Jerome's works the cataloguer listed a copy of the *De Viris Illustribus* with its continuation by Gennadius. This text was, in effect, the earliest bibliography; it lists famous writers and all the books they wrote, and perhaps the keeper of the library at Reichenau used it to check off what he still needed to fill his store of books.

Occasionally, in these early inventories, we get descriptions of script. The earliest lists for St Wandrille Abbey record books in 'Romana littera scriptum' which I take to mean uncials. The famous St Gall catalogue of the 9th century begins with 'libri scottici scripti' and a similar phrase was used around 1200 at Rebais Abbey (founded in the 7th century). Scottish script means books in what we call Irish or Insular minuscule: it may be that the cataloguer was unable to make sense of this weird writing or that it was the simplest way to distinguish one copy of the text from another.

As libraries got larger the need to tell volumes apart must have got more acute. The difficulty of course comes with duplicates; and in liturgical services and in a monastery school multiple copies of texts were essential. One solution to this problem was worked out at Christ Church, Canterbury, and survives in a fragment of a 12th-century catalogue of the manuscripts used for teaching in the cloisters. The volumes were each assigned a symbol which was written both on the flyleaf of the book and in the library catalogue.[17] These symbols were sometimes letters of the alphabet or geometric or abstract devices unique to each copy of every book. It cannot have been a very satisfactory way of checking off the books as the symbols are non-verbal, but it shows the librarians addressing what was to become a major problem as their collections became larger.

Until about 1100, the number of texts was ultimately finite and collections of books were probably stored in chests. A pleasant image of a small library emerges from the catalogue of Montier-en-Der in Burgundy: the monks record that when their abbot Adson set off for the Holy Land in 993 they rummaged 'in arca eius' and found 23 books.[18] Romanesque bookbindings, when they survive intact, generally have little tabs at each end of the spine so that a book kept fore-edge downwards could be lifted out of a chest, and often they have titles of the books written along the full-length of the spine. Bindings are generally not described in Romanesque inventories because the spine was probably all that was visible in the box. When even a really major library comprised dozens but not necessarily hundreds of books it cannot have been especially difficult to locate individual volumes. Soon this was to change. The 12th-century renaissance and the birth of the universities brought about a rapid increase in the number of texts available. Librarians were faced with bewildering problems of storing and making available new books. Bookshelves must have been one development. The 12th century took delight in creating order out of confusion, and in this century of encyclopaedias and theological and legal dictionaries it is not surprising that library catalogues became very common too.

Most 12th-century libraries catalogued their books by subjects, and this may in part be because that is how books were stored. Different parts of a monastery would need different books. The compiler of the catalogue of Reading Abbey lists the places where he found books.[19] With the catalogue and a plan of the ruins of the monastery, one can trace his route as he worked around from the cloister to a chapel off the cloister, then up a passage out to the guest-house, the infirmary, the abbot's lodging, and back into the cloister and through the refectory, and round to the abbey church. In each there were appropriate manuscripts, entered in this order into the catalogue. A seeker of books would know to go to the outbuilding or set of cupboards where the type of texts he wanted were stored. By the Gothic period institutions were bringing books together into special rooms constructed or adapted as libraries.

For the first time we find library catalogues arranged in alphabetical order of authors or by titles of anonymous works. (This method is used by most librarians today.) There are two Romanesque catalogues of Corbie, for instance. The first, of the 11th century, lists books as they were found in the cupboards, 'hi codices reperti sunt in armario', but the catalogue of a century later lists manuscripts by their authors 'in bibliotheca Corbeiensi ... imprimis codices beati Augustini': works of Augustine followed those of Ambrose, Aubert, Acts of the Apostles, Athanasius, Arator, Avitus, Anneius Florus, Alexander the Great, Alaric, Aristotle, Bede, Boethius, Basil...[20] Modern purists of alphabetisation may raise eyebrows at the sequence of second letters but it must have been quite new and a delight for monks seeking individual texts among over 300 at Corbie. Similarly the 'Brevis annotatio librorum' of manuscripts at St Bertin in the later 12th century is arranged by authors Augustine, Ambrose, Aldhelm, Alcuin, Almarius, Appodius, Arator, Bede, Bâsil, Boethius...[21] There were over 300 volumes at St Bertin too, more perhaps than a librarian could be expected to remember without an index.

In fact, 12th- and even 13th-century alphabetical catalogues are rare. By the 14th century they became much more common. Libraries may have had card indexes of some sort, or at very least slips of paper or vellum which could be shuffled into order before they were transcribed. The advantage of a card catalogue is that one can go on adding to it, a task much harder when the text is copied out continuously. Sometimes scribes left spaces in the catalogues for subsequent insertion of later acquisitions in their right places in the sequence. This is a problem in using an old printed edition of a medieval catalogue: editors have not always distinguished where space was left in the original or even whether entries are by the original scribe and whether by an early librarian making insertions.

One solution adopted at Canterbury and Durham and many other places in the later 12th century is to list the books by subject as well as possible and thereafter to accession new books as a separate sequence according to the names of their donors. Thus at Durham in the middle of the 12th century books were listed loosely by subject – clutches of St Augustine, Bede, Priscian, books in Anglo-Saxon, classical texts, and so forth – and then subsequent acquisitions appear by donor:

Hii sunt libri quos Magister Herebertus medicus dedit sancto Cuthberto
Liber febrium Ysaac, qui dicitur liber Constantini de febribus.
Liber simplicis medicinae in uno volumine.
Liber pantegni...
Libri Reginaldi
Isidorus ethimologiarum.
Sacramenta Hugonis.
Sermones G. Babuin.
Breviarium cum missale
Libri Laurentii Prioris
Psalterium glosatum secundum magistrum Anselmum.
Psalterium aliud secundum magistrum Ivonem...[22]

This method must have flattered donors and avoided constant re-shelving. It accords us a glimpse too of some of the earliest privately-owned book collections. At Canterbury, as far as one can judge from the catalogue of around 1300, most of one side of the library was then shelved by authors and by subject (including all the early books) but the second side of the library was mostly arranged by donors, beginning in the first book press with the books bequeathed by Thomas Becket (martyred in 1170), followed by those of his friend Herbert of Bosham (*d.c.*1193–4), then those of Ralph of Sarre (*d.*1194), and then those of Richard of Salisbury who had been chaplain to Thomas Becket in exile, and so forth.[23] It sounds as though the books had not been substantially rearranged since the rebuilding of Christ Church in the late 12th century. One could imagine that the library was brought into order some time around 1170, and that new acquisitions from archbishop Thomas Becket and his companions and successors meant moving the book presses to one side to introduce more furniture for acquisitions after Becket's death, and that 130 years later, when the catalogue was assembled according to what was on the shelves, the second side was full.

Though the orderly arranging and listing of volumes presented difficulties for a medieval librarian, it was nothing to a problem which bewildered medieval librarians quite as much as it does modern palaeographers and incunabulists confronting medieval books. This is the practice of binding up groups of little texts into one fat volume. It was very common especially in Germany and England. Many Middle English texts, for instance, were planned as slim booklets to be assembled and bound up in multiple manuscripts. The practice survived in those 17th- and even 18th-century collections of English pamphlets. *Sammelbände* are a characteristic feature in Germany both of medieval manuscripts and of early printing. A medieval book may contain two or three works of Albertus Magnus, one by Peraldus, one ascribed to Gregory but perhaps by Cassiodorus, and several anonymous treatises on the virtues and vices and on the Sacrament of the Mass. How, in an orderly alphabetical catalogue, can you list such a book?

Some medieval manuscripts have lists of contents added by their librarian on the flyleaf or at the top of the first page. Many cataloguers doubtless simply transcribed these lists. The Canterbury catalogue has the words '*in hoc vol.cont.*' after the entry for the first text, and follows this by listing other treatises contained there too, but it is difficult to know from the catalogue where the contents of one volume stop and those of the next begin. Thus if the catalogue says:

Liber urinarum Egidii.
   In hoc vol.cont.:
Platearius.
Liber urinarum Ysaac.
Logica vetus

are there one or two or even three volumes ? In this case, M.R. James suggested two, three little medical texts in one volume and the book on logic separately, but this is a guess.[24] Perhaps to a medieval reader it hardly mattered as long as he knew the sequence on the shelf. The Pomposa catalogue of 1093 is preceded by an explanation that the first titles in the listing of multiple texts are indicated with a mark like a 'T' and subsequent components are shown by a mark like a capital gamma (an 'F' without the middle stroke). A further difficulty of composite texts was that if the reader wanted to consult a minor work of St Bonaventura but this text was in the middle of a volume consisting mainly of Nicolaus of Dinkelsbühl and which was therefore listed under Nicolaus, there would have to be a cross-reference from among the Bonaventura entries referring the inquirer to an entry under Nicolaus many pages further on. It makes for immense complications for the cataloguer. By the late 15th-century the cataloguer of St Augustine's in

Canterbury had this quite under control with detailed references backwards and forwards to texts elsewhere. Thus there were four glossed copies of Deuteronomy, all with other texts bound in:

Deuteronom' glo.*et in eodem libro Ruth glo.Radulphi.*
Deuteronom' glo.Roberti *et in eodem libro passio*
    sancti thome martiris.
Deuteronom' glo.*non hic quia supra in levitico glo.*
Deuteronom' sine glo.*non hic quia infra in Cantica*
    canticorum glo.cum A.

The first entry is picked up again eight entries further on ('Ruth glo.*non hic quia supra in deuteronom' glo.Radulphi*') the second entry is cross-referenced over 1400 entries later ('Passio sancti Thome martiris Cant' Archiepiscopi *supra in deutronomio glo.Roberti*'), and the third and fourth entries are properly entered under glossed copies of Leviticus and the Song of Songs respectively.[25]

Anonymous texts are another problem in a catalogue arranged by authors, not made easier by the fact that medieval books do not have title-pages and often quite simply begin their texts on the first page without a heading. An author's name would be especially useful for a cataloguer arranging books alphabetically. The Corbie catalogue alphabetises 312 books by author from 'A' to 'V', ending despairingly (and neatly coinciding it with the end of the alphabet) 'Viginti et quatuor libri sine titulis'.[26] He had left the problems to the end, and still could not place them. It was fashionably modest in the middle ages when you were writing a book or telling a story to claim that it was based on the work of another well-respected author. Furthermore, it was probably easier to get a text published and sold if you said that it was by St Bernard, for instance, rather than by an unknown friend of yours. Medieval literary history is full of misattributions and we now invent authors like Pseudo-Dionysius the Areopagite. Moral and mystical treatises and sermons were especially liable to be coupled with the names of different authors in different manuscripts, and the monumental researches of the late Professors Bloomfield and Schneyer[27] and others in their respective areas have not yet untangled many of the matchings of authors with texts and vice versa. Pity the struggling medieval librarian without such bibliographies!

I began this paper with references from French royal inventories and from the early Carolingian title-lists of books in monastic treasuries. They described the physical appearance of the volumes. There is, of course, a basic difference in the purpose of the catalogue. An inventory is for the use of the *owner*. A cross-referenced author catalogue is for the use of a *reader*. An administrator of a library needs a tally of how many books he is responsible for, and he must recognise one volume from another when he checks them off: he is likely to note the binding but has no need for a fuller list of contents. A student, however, needs to know whether a certain text is in the library and how to find it quickly, and to him the physical appearance of the book and the name of the donor is of no consequence except in so far as it speeds up the location of a volume.

Until the 14th century bindings are seldom mentioned in catalogues of scholarly libraries. After that the colours of the bindings are sometimes cited, perhaps because books were now kept on display shelves; such an aid to recognition would have been of no use in the old days of dark book-boxes. The papal library at Avignon was listed in May 1369 with many references to coloured leather bindings, tanned leather, dirty red leather, red velvet with silver clasps, and so forth.[28] Similarly, coloured bindings are noted by the monk William Charite in his late 15th-century catalogue of Leicester Abbey.[29] Pierre de Virey who catalogued the library of his abbey of Clairvaux in May 1472 clearly took a bibliophile's delight in some of the antiquarian books in his care; for no reason apparently, other than the joy of manuscripts, he slips in adjectives for handsome books, mostly Romanesque:

Ung tresbeau volume moult bien escript de
  belle grande lettre . . .
D'asses ancienne lettre bien enluminé sans or . . .
Ung autre volume relié en parchemin de bonne
  lettre courrant . . .[30]

In the last two centuries of the middle ages we find the most gigantic library catalogues addressing all problems of identification at once, combining a physical description of the book to distinguish it from all other copies, together with lists of contents, the various possible citations of author, and indexing systems that will allow any text in any volume in an enormous library to be located in minutes.

Prototypes of these catalogues are found in the series of huge inventories of the Sorbonne library dating from soon before 1290 to 1338. The vastness of the book collections there and needs of the busiest university in the world must have necessitated many innovations.[31] There were over a thousand volumes in the Sorbonne library in 1290 and there were 1722 volumes by 1338. Scholars from all over Europe must have seen how these were catalogued. Some 330 were listed shelf by shelf as chained in the *magna libraria*, in effect the 'reference only' collection. It is arranged first as the books were on the shelves which were lettered 'A' to 'Z', and then 'AB', 'AC' and 'AD'; it then re-lists the books all over again according to their subjects. The *parva libraria* contained the gigantic student lending library. It is divided into 59 subject headings, according to the reading-lists of the university faculties of Arts, Medicine, Theology and Law. Some books are missing because they have been moved across to the chained library but the recurrent word 'defficit' attests to losses. A typical entry is:

Item Tullius de amicicia, ex legato magistri Egidii de Tillia, Incipit in 2° fol.*vite*, Precium XII den.[32]

Thus this copy of Cicero's *De Amicitia*, bequeathed by Master Gilles du Theil, was valued at 12 pence, the sum a borrower would forfeit if he failed to return it. The individual copy was identified by citing the first word of the text on the manuscript's second leaf.

This system of citing the opening words of the second leaf was invaluable for administrators of a collection because no hand-written book is likely to reach its second page at exactly the same syllable in the same word as any other copy. Probably from its use in the Sorbonne catalogue, it came to be used widely in

library catalogues in England and France, though rarely in Germany. Very many
15th-century catalogues follow book titles with '2' and a tiny 'o' (for secundo)
'fol.', then the key word. The antiquary John Nichols who first described the
Leicester abbey catalogue observed but did not understand these references;
puzzled, he remarked what a lot of books in the library seemed to consist of only
two leaves.[33] Sometimes the matching of *secundo folios* alone is sufficient to be able
now to ascribe a surviving manuscript to the possession of an abbey in whose
catalogue it is recorded.

One of the most efficient catalogues of the 14th century is that of Dover Priory
in 1389.[34] Its author John Whytefeld certainly deserves mention among our
pioneer bibliographers. It is in three quite distinct parts. The first is a shelf-list of
the books, like that of the Sorbonne, with short titles and pressmarks, opening
words of an identifying leaf (but not always the second), the number of leaves in
the volume, and the number (but not the nature) of the different texts in each
volume. Then the catalogue begins all over again. This time it lists the bibliographical contents of every book (with folio numbers), giving authors, titles and
opening words of every component part of the book. Finally the Dover catalogue
gives an alphabetical index. It is a really extraordinary document, and it records
450 books with a precision that satisfied everyone. All but a couple of the 25
extant books from Dover Priory can be found in it. Furthermore, the compiler
explains his purpose in producing three parallel sections: 'The object [he says] is
that the first part may supply information to the precentor of the house concerning the number of the books and the complete knowledge of them; that the
second part may stir up studious brethren to eager and frequent reading; and that
the third may point out the way to the speedy finding of individual treatises by the
scholars'.[35] This sums up the concerns of any modern library today: firstly, the
administration, secondly, the general public and, thirdly, students. In the Dover
catalogue too we can glimpse the shelf arrangements from the pressmarks. There
were nine *distinctiones*, or book presses, labelled alphabetically, each divided into
seven shelves numbered in roman numerals from the bottom upwards. The
monks usually fitted about seven to ten books on each shelf.

Even more precision on library furniture can be gleaned from the library
catalogue of Heiligenkreuz, near Vienna. The catalogue is datable between 1363
and 1374, and opens (in Latin), 'when you go into the library at Heiligenkreuz
you find three presses of which each has ten rows or shelves from top to bottom.
The first, on the left-hand side, has ten books on the top shelf, nine on the second
shelf down, ten on the third, nine on the fourth, nine on the fifth . . .'[36] and so on,
describing exactly the 91 books on the presses on the left, 101 in the presses in the
middle, and 117 in the press on the right.

The two Canterbury libraries were also in what were perhaps similar presses.
Those at Christ Church evidently had 12 or 13 shelves to a press but they often
only had three or four volumes to a shelf. Presumably the books lay on their sides.
At St Augustine's there were a maximum of six shelves to a book press with up to
a dozen or so manuscripts to a shelf. The library catalogue of the Vienna Domini-
cans copied in 1513[37] describes books in double-sided desks labelled alphabeti-

cally and subdivided into front and back, each with two shelves: there were an average of 10 books on the upper shelves and 16 on the lower shelves, and so one must imagine the presses with sloping tops where fewer books could be displayed than could be piled below.

The last catalogues of the middle ages include printed books. Medieval librarians mixed them up with manuscripts quite indiscriminately. The early 16th-century catalogue of the monks' library at Syon Abbey describes just over 1400 volumes and one can only admire its editor Mary Bateson who in 1898 realised that the opening words of the second leaves often corresponded to those of known incunabula, and by the enormous task of checking every text in the catalogue against every extant early printed edition she identified some 400 printed books which were at Syon.[38] This is valuable information for the history of the early book trade in England. Wynkyn de Worde, incidentally gave them two books.[39] One can note too that Erhard Ratdolt, the incunabular printer from Augsburg and Venice, gave a substantial library to the Carmelite convent of St Anna in Augsburg in 1484 and 1493 and his books were listed in the convent's library catalogue before 1497.[40]

In conclusion let us take one catalogue entry from the vast late 15th-century catalogue of the Carthusians of Salvatorberg at Erfurt. Among many hundreds of manuscripts cross-indexed and shelved in their library was a book at the end of the bottom shelf of the press containing Bibles:

Biblia rubea impressa et integra Moguntina et multum correcta secundum ordinem Carthusiensium sine Hebreorum nominum interpretatione.[41]

If nothing else, the library catalogue has probably revealed the earliest bibliographical description of a Gutenberg Bible.

References

1. G. Becker, *Catalogi Bibliothecarum Antiqui*, Bonn, 1885 (reprinted, Hildesheim and New York 1973); T. Gottlieb, *Über Mittelalterliche Bibliotheken*, Leipzig, 1890; an excellent survey of medieval library catalogues, with bibliography, is A. Derolez, *Les Catalogues de Bibliothèques*, Turnhout, 1979 (*Typologie des Sources du Moyen Age Occidental*, fasc. XXXI), and I acknowledge its help.

2. *Catalogue Général des manuscrits des bibliothèques publiques des départements*, Paris, 1849 *et seq.*; L. Delisle, *Le Cabinet des manuscrits de la Bibliothèque Impériale*, Paris, 1868-81.

3. *Mittelalterliche Bibliothekskataloge Deutschlands und der Schweiz*, 4 vols. in 8 parts, Munich, 1918-79; *Mittelalterliche Bibliothekskataloge Österreichs*, 5 vols. in 6 parts, Vienna, 1915-71.

4. The standard edition is L. Delisle, *Recherches sur la Librairie de Charles V*, 2 vols., Paris, 1907 (part 2 includes the inventories of Charles VI and the Duc de Berry).

5. *Ibid*, II, p.*177, no.1081.

6. *Ibid*, II, p.*48, no.271.

7. *Ibid*, II, p.*249, no.156.

8. *Ibid*, II, pp.*10–11, nos.46–7; both survive: the Ingebourg Psalter at Chantilly, and the Psalter of St Louis (B.N.ms.lat.10525).

9. *Ibid*, p.*226, no.18.

10. It is Paris, B.N.ms.lat.8824 (E. Temple, *Anglo-Saxon Manuscripts, 900–1066*, 1976, no.82, figs. 208–9).

11. Delisle, *Recherches*, pp.*226–7, no.19; Becket must surely have owned a liturgical Psalter though no copy was among the residue of his personal library at Christ Church, Canterbury, in the early 14th century (M.R. James, *The Ancient Libraries of Canterbury and Dover*, Cambridge, 1903, pp.82–85, nos.783–853).

12. Becker, no.11, pp.24–29.

13. *Ibid*, no.36, pp.,79–81.

14. *Ibid*, no.5, p.4.

15. *Ibid*, no.37, p.82.

16. *Ibid*, no.6, pp.4–13; Lehmann, *Mittelalt. Bibliothekskat. Deutschlands und der Schwiez*, I, 1918, no.49, pp.240–252.

17. James, *Ancient Libraries*, pp.xxxii–iii and 3–12.

18. Becker, no.41, pp.126–7.

19. S. Barfield, 'Lord Fingall's Cartulary of Reading Abbey', *English Historical Review*, III, 1888, pp.117–23.

20. Becker, nos.55 and 79, pp.139–40 and 185–92.

21. Becker, no.77, pp.181–84.

22. Becker, no.117, pp.239–45; Master Herbert the doctor gave a whole library of medical textbooks (R.A.B. Mynors, *Durham Cathedral Manuscripts*, Durham, 1939, p.46).

23. James, *Ancient Libraries*, pp.82 ('*Incipit secunda demonstratio cum contentis*') *et seq.*

24. *Ibid*, p.123, nos. 1449–50.

25. *Ibid*, p.202, nos.16–19; p.203, no.24; p.375, no.18; p.202, no.9; and p.204, no.1.

26. Becker, p.191, last entry.

27. M.W. Bloomfield et al., *Incipits of Latin Works on the Virtues and Vices, 1100–1500 A.D.*, Cambridge (Mass.), 1979; J.B. Schneyer, *Repertorium des Lateinischen Sermones des Mittelalters (Beiträge zur Geschichte der Philosophie und Theologie des Mittelalters*, XLIII, i–ix), Münster, 1969–79.

28. M. Faucon, *La Librairie des Papes d'Avignon*, Paris, 1886, 'cooperto corio rubeo', 'coopertum corio nigro', 'cooperto postibus sine pello', etc.

29. M.R. James, 'Catalogue of the library of Leicester Abbey', *Trans. Leicestershire Archaeol. Soc.*, XIX, 1936–7, pp.118–61 and 378–440, and XXI, 1939–41, pp.1–88, 'in ass.cum alb.co.', 'cum nigro coop.et impresso', 'in nudis ass.', etc.

30. A. Vernet and J.-F. Genest, *La Bibliothèque de l'Abbaye de Clairvaux du XIIe au XVII siècle*, Paris, 1979, nos.459, 599 and 1201.

31. R.H. Rouse, 'The Early Library of the Sorbonne', *Scriptorium*, XXI, 1967, pp.42–71 and 227–51; the catalogues are printed in Delisle, *Cabinet des Manuscrits*, III, pp.9–114.

32. *Ibid*, p.62, no.37.

33. James, 'Leicester Abbey', p.118.

34. James, *Ancient Libraries*, pp.407–496.

35. *Ibid*, p.410.
36. T. Gottlieb, *Mittelalterliche Bibliothekskataloge Österreichs*, I, *Niederösterreich*, Vienna, 1915, p.24.
37. *Ibid*, pp.293–414.
38 M. Bateson, *Catalogue of the Library of Syon Monastery, Isleworth*, Cambridge, 1898, esp.pp.vii-viii.
39. *Ibid*, p.9, no.A.75, and p.103, no.M.30.
40. P. Ruf, *Mittelaterliche Bibliothekskataloge Deutschlands und der Schweiz*, III, i, *Bistum Augsburg*, Munich, 1932, pp.30–31.
41. P. Lehmann, *Mittelalterliche Bibliothekskataloge Deutschlands und der Schweiz*, II, *Bistum Mainz, Erfurt*, Munich, 1928, p.273.

Discussion following the paper

Contributors: Gwyn Walters, Katherine Swift, Robin Myers, Keith Maslen, Michael Harris, Esther Potter, Elisabeth Leedham-Green, Michael Winship, Peter Stockham, Charles Rivington, Mirjam Foot.

The speaker was asked about the existence of medieval cataloguing rules. He said that he knew of no medieval instructions on how to catalogue books but said advice on how the catalogues themselves were to be used was often given in prologues of late medieval catalogues. There was considerable discussion on the question of non-matching manuscripts. Following on from the medieval practice of citing the opening words of the second leaf in order to distinguish one copy of a text from another, Katherine Swift suggested one would expect more duplication since it would surely have been easier for a scribe to copy line by line; Christopher de Hamel gave as one reason why it didn't happen that they didn't want books to be identical, something that we, in the age of the printed book, easily overlook. This led on to discussion of variable page sizes and differing sizes of handwriting. Keith Maslen, claiming to share a sheep-farming nationality with the speaker, introduced a light-hearted note in commenting that sheep varied in size so that the skins from which book pages were made would not be standard either. Christopher de Hamel agreed and noted that it was the shape of sheep which finally dictated the shape, oblong rather than square, of book paper, so that we now have upright books with strong spines, easier to read than square books.

Esther Potter commented that the Romans dictated to scribes; there seemed to be no evidence, Christopher de Hamel said, that medieval books were produced from dictation; medieval illustrations show scribes copying from an exemplar and when medieval books were made in monasteries, only a single copy would often be called for. Questions by Katherine Swift and others regarding the purpose of inventories and of priced catalogues led to comment which the speaker has incorporated in his paper.

On the subject of medieval collecting of catalogues Christopher de Hamel said that the Franciscans were evidently collecting the catalogues of other libraries in the 13th century, and in the mid-14th century Henry of Kirkestede (the so-called 'Boston of Bury') compiled a vast and unfinished union catalogue of manuscripts in British libraries, his *Catalogus Scriptorum Ecclesiae*. Mirjam Foot's question about catalogue descriptions of decorated edges led to comment on the imprecise description of colour in medieval bookbindings in catalogues and this in turn led to discussion of the linguistic interpretation of medieval words for colours.

Anthony Wood, John Bagford and Thomas Hearne as bibliographers

T.A. BIRRELL

Introduction

THE THEME of this year's conference – 'Pioneers in Bibliography' – is paradoxically very relevant to the present state of bibliography. It is not only most salutary to remind ourselves that we are pygmies on the shoulders of giants; it is also important to realise that bibliography has hitherto always been thought of as an ancillary science and that nowadays there is a dangerous tendency for it to develop into an autotelic activity. The three men whom I have chosen to talk about most certainly did not consider bibliography as an end in itself: the words bibliographer and bibliography, in our sense of the terms, did not exist in the English language, and neither did the concept. The *Oxford English Dictionary* records the first instances of 'bibliographer' and 'bibliography' in 1814, in Dibdin's preface to the *Bibliotheca Spenceriana*.[1]

Anthony Wood was an historian and a biographer; John Bagford was a library agent and a 'book runner' (I shall explain the term in due course); and Thomas Hearne was a librarian, a textual critic and a textual editor. They all three belong to a period at the end of the 17th century and beginning of the 18th century before there was any substantive achievement in explicit bibliographical description – in other words before Joseph Ames, *Typographical Antiquities* (1749) and Georg Wolfgang Panzer, *Annales Typographici* (1793). As I hope to show, Wood, Bagford and Hearne all had to acquire their bibliographical expertise in a very haphazard way. You must try to think yourselves back into the world with no *STC*, no *Wing*, no *Lowndes*, no *BMC*, no *BMSTC*, no *GK III*, no Brunet, no Graesse, no McKerrow, no Gaskell, no Bowers. Wood, Bagford and Hearne are three very attractive human beings, and they are three men who, from their own times to the present day, have been undervalued and denigrated, or else, which is worse, condescended to and patronised.

Anthony Wood (1632–1695)

Let us start with Anthony Wood, who devoted his entire life to the glorification of Oxford University, on an income of about £30 a year, the salary of a well-paid country curate. According to Anthony Powell, the biographer of John Aubrey, Wood is 'a figure whose many unattractive characteristics make a just account of his activities somewhat difficult to compile...an uneasy, bad tempered man...he has a violent, uncouth manner of writing...peevish, feminine...parsimonious, quarrelsome and backbiting... one of those uninviting pedants... a lonely unpopular recluse.'[2] I need hardly say that that is not my interpretation of the portrait presented in Andrew Clark's magnificent five-volume edition of Wood's *Life and Times* (Oxford, 1891–1900). But our concern here is not with amateur psychoanalysis, but with Wood's concrete achievement.

Having completed his monumental history of Oxford University, and before it even started going through the press, Wood conceived the idea of the *Athenae Oxonienses*, the bio-bibliographical record of Oxford writers. The scale of the thing was, for its time, unique. We take Wood's *Athenae* so much for granted, we are so quick and eager to point out in our learned footnotes where Wood was wrong, that we fail to realise the true nature of his achievement. A glance through the bibliographies of bio-bibliographical dictionaries in Jöcher's *Allgemeines Gelehrten-Lexicon* (1750) will quickly show that there is nothing in Europe before Wood to equal him in scale of detail both biographically and bibliographically. The first book to approach the scale of Wood's *Athenae* was Johann Moller's *Cimbria Literata*, a magnificent bio-bibliography of Schleswig Holstein, published in 1744, and this was followed by innumerable bio-bibliographical dictionaries in the 18th and 19th centuries. The sheer daring of Wood's undertaking becomes apparent when we realise that all he had in the way of reference books in print were Bale's *Scriptores Britanniae* (1559), Pits's *De Illustribus Angliae Scriptoribus* (1619) and Thomas Hyde's Bodleian Catalogue of 1674 – and the latter is conspicuously weak in ephemera and in creative English literature.

Not all of Wood's notes and manuscript materials for *Athenae* have survived, but we have enough to be able to reconstruct his working methods.[3] His first means of acquiring information was by word of mouth: he cultivated friends and acquaintances who could supply him with information. Wood's *Life and Times* shows him as a convivial diner-out (*pace* Mr Powell, Wood was not unpopular and lonely, though deafness in later life restricted his social contacts), but Wood was never so convivial that he forgot to record in his diary whatever bio-bibliographical scraps of information could be gleaned from his companions.

The second method of acquiring information was by correspondence. In the early 1670s, as soon as he had finished the history of Oxford University, Wood began to send out explicit questionnaires for the *Athenae*: he sent them to his friends and, where necessary, asked for the questionnaires to be passed on to other informants with whom he was not acquainted. When the material came in, it was collated, checked as best he could, and then incorporated into the *Athenae* on a scissors-and-paste method. One must be careful of attributing to Wood's 'quaint' style every phrase and expression that is found in the *Athenae*: Wood very often takes over sentences and phrases verbatim from his informants.

Wood's third bibliographical source was catalogues, manuscript and printed, of every sort that he could lay his hands on. He used Maunsell's *Catalogue* (1595), to which he has provided a manuscript index, William London's *Catalogue* (1657–60), George Tokefield's *Catalogue* (1664) of books entered in the Stationers' Register (Wood's copy is unique), and Robert Clavell's *Term Catalogues* (1673–80). Furthermore, Wood has a magnificent run of more than 80 auction sale catalogues from the first sale of Lazarus Seaman (1676).[4] Wood systematically read and abstracted from these catalogues page by page and item by item. Occasionally he records his irritation when an auction catalogue is defective, e.g. 'In this catalogue are the years of certain books, when printed, omitted, especially if the title cannot come within the compass of the line'; or again: 'No Christian names to the authors in this catalogue and therefore for my use not worth a scan' – but he *has* in fact scanned it and made several notes. He also uses booksellers' catalogues: William Jaggard's 1618 catalogue (Wood's copy is unique), Humphrey Moseley's catalogue of 1653, and two catalogues of law books by Thomas Bassett (1673 and 1682) which Wood has cross-checked with the auction sale catalogues. Several of Wood's catalogues of plays have been used by W.W. Greg in his *Bibliography of English Printed Drama* (1939–59): Greg presented his photostats of Wood's catalogues to the British Library – Greg is the only case I know of a man who had his photostats gilt-edged.

The range of Wood's catalogues is well illustrated by his ownership of a very remarkable production, *The Lamps of the Law and the Lights of the Gospel*, by Grass and Hay Wythers (1658). This is a perfectly genuine catalogue of the literature of the Civil War and Commonwealth period, compiled by Wood's friend Thomas Blount of the Inner Temple. The criterion of inclusion is the oddity of the titles – Thomas Blount had an eye for the odd and the curious in many things.[5] *The Lamps of the Law* lists titles of books by Isaac Pennington, William Dewesberry, Francis Howgil, George Fox, James Nailer, Richard Hubberthorn, Dennis Hollister, George Whitehead and Thomas Lawson: Blount is probably the earliest bibliographer of Quakers and sectaries. There was no index of the Thomason Tracts available till the end of the 17th century,[6] so that for Wood *The Lamps of the Law* was the next best thing. There are only two printed copies of *The Lamps of the Law* in existence, and Wood owned both of them.

Apart from his sets of catalogues, Wood acquired many other sorts of rare ephemera. But he did not collect as a mere collector, as a bibliophile or as an antiquarian. He collected ephemera as a bibliographer, because ephemera were not preserved in the Bodleian or in the Oxford college libraries. Primarily, he collected every scrap of Oxford printing that he could lay his hands on: where necessary he annotates it with the date and the author, and identifies the allusions. You have only to read through Falconer Madan's *Oxford Books* (Oxford 1895–1931) to see how often Madan uses Wood for information on rare or complex material. Apart from Oxford printing, Wood's collections of ephemera are listed by Andrew Clark in his introduction to the *Life and Times*: ballads and broadsides, almanacks and chapbooks, pamphlets on God's judgements, on prophecies, on witches and ghosts, on floods and fires, on murders, on rogues and thieves, on tobacco, ale, wine, tea and coffee, on women and marriage. The arrangement under headings is simply a finding device, it is not because Wood is concentrating on certain topics like a bibliophile. What interests Wood is the preservation and registration of any and every sort of letterpress. It is a bibliographical concept which Wood shares with John Bagford and with Dr K.F. Pantzer, and which was not fully accepted by the compilers of the first *STC* and which apparently is not accepted by Dr K.W. Humphreys as future policy for the National Library.[7]

In order to give an idea of Wood at work in the *Athenae*, I have chosen the bio-bibliography of an obscure nonentity, Simon Harward:

SIMON HARWARD, whose native place is too me as yet unknown, became one of the Chaplains of *New* Coll. in 1577, was incorporated Bach. of Arts the same year, as he had stood elsewhere, but in what Univ. or Academy, it appears not. Afterwards he proceeded in Arts as a Member of the said Coll., left the University soon after, and became a Preacher at *Warrington* in *Lancashire.*, Thence he removed to *Bansted* in *Surrey* about the latter end of *Q. Elizabeth*, and thence, having a rambling head, to *Tanridge* in the same County, where I find him in 1604, to be a Schoolmaster, and, as it seems, a practitioner in Physic. His works are these,

Two godly Sermons preached at *Manchester* in *Lanc.* The first containeth a reproof of the subtile practices of dissembling Neuters, and politic Wordlings, on *Rom.* 10.19. The other, a charge and instruction to all unlearned, negligent, and dissolute Ministers, on *Luke* 20.2. *Lond.* 1582. oct.

Exhortation to the common People to seek their amendment by Prayer with God. – Printed with the two Sermons before-mentioned. He purposed then also to write the second part of the aforesaid Text on *Rom.* 10.19. but because he had occasion to intreat more at large of that article of Justification in another Work, which he did determine to publish, he then thought good to omit it for that time.

Sermons, *viz.* one preached at *Crowhurst*, on *Psal.* 1 ver.1. – Lond. 1592. oct. and another on 1 *Sam.* 12.19. – printed 1590. in oct.&c.

Solace for a Soldier and Sailor, containing an Apology out of the Word of God, how we are to esteem of the valiant attempts of Noblemen and Gentlemen of *England*, which incurr so many dangers on the Seas to abridge the proud Power of *Spain*. Lond. 1592.qu.

Phlebotomy: Or, a Treatise of letting Blood. *Lond.* 1601. oct.

Discourse concerning the Soul and Spirit of Man, wherein is described the Essence and Dignity thereof, &c. *Lond.* 1614. oct.

Discourse of the several kinds and causes of Lightning. Written by occasion of a fearful Lightning, 17 Nov. 1606. Which in short time burnt the Spire-steeple of *Blechingley* in *Surrey*, and in the same, melted into infinite fragments a godly ring of Bells. Lond. 1607, in three sh. in qu.

A most profitable new Treatise from approved experience of the art of propagating Plants. *Lond.* 1623.qu. This was published after the Author's death (as it seems) by one *Will. Lawson*, at the end of his *New Orchard and Garden*, &c. What other things our Author *S. Harward* hath written, I cannot yet find; not do I know how to trace him to his Grave, because he died not at *Tanridge*, as a worthy Knight of that Town (Sir *W. Hayward*) hath informed me, but removed thence to another place, which I think was *Blechingley* before-mentioned.

On the biographical side, Wood's epithet 'having a rambling head' is presumably a simple deduction from the fact that Harward moved around the country (Harward's addresses are derived from the prelims of his books), and also from the fact that, as well as publishing sermons, Harward wrote on such diverse subjects as botany and phlebotomy. Wood quite openly confesses that his knowledge of the man is incomplete, and tells us whom he has consulted, i.e. Sir William Hayward of Tanridge (in fact, Wood got his friend Dr Thomas 'Tograi' Smith of Magdalen, later the Cottonian librarian, to write to Hayward in the first instance).[8] Most important of all, Wood has a hunch that Harward's bibliography is incomplete, and frankly tells us so.

On the bibliographical side, Hyde's Bodleian catalogue of 1674 was not much help to Wood: it only recorded Harward's *Art of Propagating Plants*, 4° Lond. 1623. Wood's comments on the *Exhortation to the Common People* are simply derived from the book itself (*STC* 12924). He has got the dates of publication wrong for the *Sermon* on 1. Sam. 12.19 (*STC* 12923.5) – 1590 instead of 1599; and also for the *Discourse concerning the Soul and Spirit of Man* (*STC* 12917) – 1614 instead of 1604. Wood has in fact only missed one of Harward's publications, *Encheiridion Morale* 8° Lond. 1596 and 1597 (*STC* 12919 and 12920). The book is rare (as indeed are all of Harward's works) and there are no extant copies recorded at Oxford: of the 1596 ed. the only extant copies are at Cambridge University, Trinity College Cambridge, Cashel (if they have not yet sold it), Folger and Huntington; and of the 1597 ed. only the Royal Library copy still exists in the British Library.

There remains Wood's reference to the *Sermon* 'preached at *Crowhurst* on *Psal.* 1, ver. 1. *Lond.* 1592. oct.' This is not recorded in *STC* at all. It is recorded in the Stationers' Register, with the title 'The Summum Bonum, or Chief Happiness of a Faithful Christian', and it is also recorded, without the title, in Maunsell's *Catalogue* (1595), from which Wood presumably derived it. Furthermore, it is also recorded, with title, in Watt's *Bibliotheca Britannica* (1824). It would be a work of supererogation to check Watt's slips in the Paisley Free Library, and it is reasonable to assume that Watt also derived his entry, directly or indirectly, from the Stationers' Register.

If you compare the entry on Harward in the *STC* of 1926 (2.3 column inches) with the entry in the *STC* of 1986 (5.2 column inches), you can see that even Pollard and Redgrave did not say the last word on Harward. Wood's single-handed effort to provide a bibliography for an obscure, rare and complicated author is a fair example of the standard of his often underrated bibliographical expertise.

John Bagford (1650–1716)

I have said that Wood owned the only two extant printed copies of *The Lamps of the Law*, but there does exist a complete manuscript transcript made by someone who realised its rarity and importance – and that someone was John Bagford.[9]

Bagford was a library agent and a book runner. The best description of a book runner is in O.F. Snelling's delightful memoirs *Rare Books and Rarer People* (1982): the breed has survived from the 17th century to the present day. The book runner has no shop or office: he haunts the booksellers' shops and the auctions and he matches up books with potential buyers. Bagford did his business in the coffee houses and taverns around Holborn and Fleet Street. If you walk down Kingsway a few yards past the entrance to Holborn Tube Station and turn left down the first dirty little alleyway that you come to, you will find the Ship Tavern, which has a board outside announcing that it was the haunt of John Bagford (unfortunately his name has been spelt as 'Bayford').

Besides being a book runner, Bagford built up a business as a high-class library agent; his three principal customers were Robert Harley, John Moore Bishop of Ely, and Sir Hans Sloane. Sloane's library was on the corner of Southampton Row, the Bishop of Ely's library was in Ely Place, Holborn, and Harley's library was at 14 York Buildings, off the Strand, between Charing Cross and the Aldwych: so the Ship Tavern was strategically situated.[10]

Bagford knew the sort of things his customers wanted. He had the run of their libraries, so he knew what they had got and what they had not got, and he tried to fill the gaps in their collections, and he bid for them at auction. The secret of his success was that each customer was, as it were, a personal friend. The correspondence with one collector, Walter Clavell, a barrister of the Middle Temple, is a good example.[11] Clavell was often out of town; he writes from Sherbourn on 1 February 1706: 'Go to Mr Cloystermans who is a dutch painter and lives at a house in the Piazza in Covent Garden (immediately upon the receipt of this) and get a catalogue of the books of architecture, painting etc. which according to an advertisement in the newspaper is to be disposed of by Auction on the 4th of this instant February, and if you find these things of value to attend the sale and take the prices of what is sold.' And he goes on to instruct Bagford to buy certain books of engravings at about 20 shillings a piece. On 13 April 1706 Clavell instructs Bagford 'wholly to conceal the catalogues you have from Holland and the intelligence with Mr Bullord (Bagford's agent in Holland) to avoid being disappointed in the buying what manuscripts shall offer there – but of this I have formerly given you a caution and therefore shall say no more at this time'. No one would dare to write to Quaritch like that – but Bagford handled his customers in his own way. Between 1686 and 1716 he was at the centre of the antiquarian booktrade.[12]

Every antiquarian bookseller has a certain amount of bibliographical expertise, so what makes Bagford special? Bagford kept records of whatever items of bibliographical interest passed through his hands. He was much more than a dealer; he used the information he collected from his trade experience for more than merely commercial purposes. He analysed the material and tried to build up from it a bibliographical methodology. The reason why Bagford's notes are so useful is precisely because he knew what was worth noting.

Most of Bagford's notes and specimens of letterpress are in the Harleian collection in the British Library. Those who have tried to use them are confronted by two difficulties. Firstly, Bagford's handwriting is appalling; and when you have deciphered it, you realise that his spelling is appalling as well: it takes some time to appreciate that 'Venus' means 'Venice'. He often employed amanuenses to copy out his notes, but that made things worse because, since they knew nothing about bibliography, they were even less able to read his handwriting than we are. Secondly, Bagford's collections in the British Library have been subjected to the most dreadful inter-departmental vandalism. Originally the manuscripts and printed titlepages and other ephemera were all kept together in the Department of Manuscripts, but then, in 1891, to the lasting shame of Richard Garnett and W. Y.

Fletcher, the printed material was ripped out of its context and transferred to the Department of Printed Books.

But if, after all that, you are prepared to read through Bagford's collections, you will certainly appreciate that the man was a true bibliographer. At the outset, it should be said that Bagford's project for a *History of Printing*, never completed, is really an irrelevance. What is important is to realise the scope of Bagford's bibliographical expertise, to try to analyse his methodology – and indeed, to recognise the fact that he *is* a methodologist.

Firstly, since he had not the advantage of Robin Myers's bibliography of *The British Booktrade*, Bagford compiled lists of books about books, under subjects; and he read them.[13] It is really surprising how much material he could find, and in quite unlikely places: it is very instructive to see the way in which he guts the most unlikely books. For instance, I often have to remind students working on the mid-17th century booktrade to look at Archbishop Ussher's letters: Bagford has read them right through and gleaned every scrap of bibliographical information.[14]

Secondly, Bagford was an avid compiler of catalogues of catalogues: he knows what catalogues are useful for what.[15]

Thirdly, in recording rare books he understands (a) the significance of *full* imprint, i.e. including address and trade sign and description of publishers' devices; (b) the significance of location of multiple copies; (c) the significance of provenance, from and to. Bagford is often accused of tearing out title pages; we must remember that he often had made quasi-facsimile title pages in manuscript, with notes of locations added at the side.[16]

Fourthly, he listed the early London printers chronologically, and indexed them according to their addresses. So E. Gordon Duff's *Century of the English Book Trade* (1905) was not the first to realise the significance of printers' addresses, and that for instance the shop at the Sign of St George in Fleet Street, next St Dunstan's Church, was occupied successively by Richard Pynson, Robert Redman, William Middleton and William Powell: Bagford had grasped that point 200 years before.[17]

Fifthly, Bagford understands the importance of state papers, wardrobe accounts, wills and other archive material for the history of early English printing.[18]

Sixthly, having dealt with early printing on a topographical and chronological basis, Bagford realises that it was more manageable to deal with other rare material on the basis of subject or theme: for instance, books on London (one of his special interests); on shorthand; on calligraphy; on music; on fencing; on war; on grammar; ballads and chapbooks; dictionaries; bibles; and so on. Or else he deals with books on specific topics, such as the Marprelate Tracts – he must have been one of the first to isolate that as a special bibliographical problem.[19]

Seventhly, Bagford was interested in the processes and appurtenances of printing: paper, ink, wood and copper engraving, and of course bookbinding (he began his working life with leather, as a shoemaker). It was Bagford who provided Howard Nixon with one of the two pieces of evidence which restored Samuel Mearne to the status of a binder – evidence which had been ignored by the atrabilious E. Gordon Duff, even though it was right under his nose.[20]

Eighthly, Bagford had a flair for sensing what was rare and what was of bibliographical significance, and recording it: it is because of that flair that his notes contain records of books that have subsequently disappeared.[21]

Bagford was not a magpie 'collector', nor a naïve 'compiler', nor a failed historian of printing. Though his collections may seem at first sight to be amorphous, what I have tried to suggest is that they reveal an acute bibliographical intelligence, a mind that was analysing the very disparate bibliographical evidence for the purpose of formulating bibliographical procedures and methodologies.

Bagford was one of the co-founders, with Humfrey Wanley, of the Society of Antiquaries. In her history of the Society of Antiquaries (1956), Dame Joan Evans gives Bagford three and a half lines: 'John Bagford was an eccentric shoemaker and collector of ballads, who cut out innumerable title pages from books as material for a history of printing. He was far from rich and died as a brother of the Charterhouse'. Bagford is worth a better epitaph than that.

Thomas Hearne (1678–1735)

The judgements on Thomas Hearne are also predominantly hostile. Cyril Wright, sometime Deputy Keeper of Manuscripts at the British Library, declares, 'his diaries are a storehouse of gossip (mostly malicious) and often inaccurate information about his contemporaries'.[22] That was because Hearne did not like Wright's hero, Humfrey Wanley. And in the recent monumental history of the University of Oxford, Stuart Piggott sneeringly refers to Hearne as 'the learned rustic ... an Oxford misfit, withdrawn into himself, he had the peasant's hoarding instinct, incurious too often of the real value of this or that scrap of knowledge that might one day be useful, the worth of the bric-à-brac with which he crowded his mind.'[23] And Harry Carter's account of Hearne's relations with the Oxford University Press is both inadequate and misleading.[24] There is only one adequate tribute to Hearne, and that is to Hearne as a medieval historian: it forms a chapter in David C. Douglas's delightful *English Scholars* (1939; 1951).

Thomas Hearne's father was a day-labourer who taught himself to read and write and became a parish clerk. One of Hearne's brothers was a gardener and his sister was a serving maid. Thomas Hearne himself began as a day-labourer but the local squire paid for his schooling and for his university education. He studied at St Edmund Hall, Oxford, and was what we might call a student research assistant to Dr John Mill, Principal of St Edmund Hall and one of the great figures in the history of New Testament scholarship in England. After taking his BA in 1699, Hearne became janitor of the Bodleian Library, and later assistant keeper at a salary of £10 a year plus tips. Hearne was a Nonjuror and refused to acknowledge William III or George I. In 1716 he was deprived of his post for refusing the Oaths of Allegiance and Abjuration, and locked out of the Bodleian. For the rest of his life he supported himself by editing medieval English historical texts and publishing them by subscription.

Bibliography, as far as Hearne is concerned, is part of his career as a librarian and a textual critic. Hearne edited and published over 40 texts. He began as a classicist with an edition of the letters of the younger Pliny (1703) and a six-volume edition of Livy (1708). Hearne had the ability to transcribe, collate, index and proof-read texts – in Latin, Greek and Old English – with phenomenal speed, phenomenal legibility and phenomenal accuracy. In his autobiography Hearne refers with pride to the New Testament collations that he did as an undergraduate for Dr Mill, and Hearne's published edition of Pliny is a remarkable piece of work for a young man of 25.[25] The most practical asset of a bibliographer is the ability to collate and edit texts with speed and accuracy – it is the combination of speed with accuracy that makes the genius. And indeed it is that combination which is the basis of Hearne's working life.

Hearne's day-to-day working life is laid before us in a chronological account set out in 145 notebooks and printed in 11 volumes as *Remarks and Collections* (Oxford 1885–1921). They are not easy to read straight through as they combine a personal diary with a workbook; it is as if you mixed up Pepys's diary with Henry Bradshaw's notebooks. Most people go to the indexes of Hearne's diary to check a particular reference, but to understand the many-sidedness of Hearne's genius, you have to read the diary straight through – all 11 printed volumes.

The early volumes show Hearne at work in the Bodleian Library, 'modelling' the books: by that he means rearranging the books on the shelves.[26] You can see in the diary how he goes along the shelves, gutting the contents of every book that he thinks useful. The most recent acquisition to the Bodleian was the library of Bishop Thomas Barlow (1607–91): Barlow often puts bibliographical notes on his books and Hearne records them in his diary. For instance, on an anonymous book against Martin Clifford, *Observations upon a Treatise intituled Of Humane Reason*, Lond. 1675,12°: Hearne notes, 'The author was Mr Edw. Stephens of Gloucestershire who had writ a great many other small pieces which are in the Bodleian Library. They are most very hard to be got, he printing them at his own charge, and so having but a very few (sometimes not above 30 or 40 copies).'[27] Like a true bibliographer, Hearne is not merely concerned with identifying anonyma: he notes the book specially because it is part of a controversy, and he notes the size of the edition. A glance at Wing confirms the rarity of many of Stephens's books.

Sometimes you will find Hearne compiling subject indexes. For instance, a list of a dozen books on mysticism, some of which are very rare and out of the way: this was in answer to a query from a country clergyman. On another occasion he compiles lists of useful authors: 'Writers to be consulted de Nummis [16 authors] ... De Epigrammatibus [15 authors] ... De Aedificiis [8 authors] ... De Statuis [2 authors] ... De Gemmis [11 authors] ... Toreumata [6 authors] ... Angeiographia [5 authors].' Or again, he notes the best edition: 'The first edition of Guillim's Heraldry is much the best, the rest having been almost spoiled by ignorant persons taking care of it.'[28] Hearne functioned as a one-man Readers' Enquiry Desk at the Bodleian.

In the case of rare books, he collates. This is his account of the notorious Oxford Rufinus of 1478: 'This book (the outer margin being cut away more at the side than at the top and bottom; and because it hath 8 leaves in one signature, as A,B,C etc.) appears like a large octavo: but is indeed a small quarto, with two sheets in one signature and one sewing: as appears, both by the Rules in the Paper [i.e. chainlines], which do not lie from top to bottom (as in folios and octavos) but cross the page from side to side . . . and by the mark of the paper [i.e. the water-mark] which is to be seen (near to the sewing) not at the top of the page (as in octavos) but near the middle of it, as in quartos . . . it appears to be printed by half sheets . . .' – and he goes on to give reasons for that.[29] Where else in the early 18th century do you find a discussion of half-sheet imposition?

Hearne understands what we should call textual tradition. On 1 June 1708 he writes to his friend John Bagford, 'In your list of old printed books 'twill be useful to tell us, if possible, what number were printed at a time. I wish also remarks were made in short form from what manuscripts the impressions were made and where the several manuscripts are now. This will be the more difficult to do, because the first editors were very negligent in directing where the manuscripts they used were lodged.'[30] That corresponds very much, I believe, to the ideals of cataloguing policy of modern incunabulists.

Another impressive example of Hearne's concern for textual tradition can be seen in his notes on Chaucer's *Canterbury Tales*, which he made to help his Nonjuror friend, John Urry of Christ Church, who was preparing an edition of Chaucer. Hearne very quickly got to the nub of the problem: by collating every manuscript and printed text of Chaucer that he could lay his hands on, Hearne realised that the text of the *Canterbury Tales* exists in more than one sequence, and that therefore Caxton's printed text only represents one textual tradition.[31]

Hearne pays scrupulous attention to signs of provenance, e.g. his notes on what was then Bodley Ms NE A.4.1: 'Several pieces of St Augustin in an old Hand on Vellam, a fair MSt. At the End, in red Letters, *Hunc librum scripsit frater Willhelmus de Wodecherche, laicus quondam conversus Pontis Roberti* . . . this Book came afterwards into the possession of John Bp. of Exeter . . . N.B. Robertsbridge was a Cistertian Abbey in Surrey built to the honour of the V. Mary. See Notitia Monastica p.224.'[32] If you look up Neil Ker's *Medieval Libraries* (1964) under Robertsbridge (pp.160 and 296) you will find the manuscript and the inscription duly recorded.

Hearne had an eye for early book-collectors: 'Apian's Inscriptions which we have in the Publick Library (Med. Seld. C.1.14) formerly belonged to Edw. Gwynn, who was certainly a most curious Collector of Books; for in the said Library I have seen divers other rare Books with his Name to them, and a certain Gentleman some years since told me he had made the same observation in some other Libraries.'[33] Edward Gwynn was the owner of the famous 1619 set of Shakespeare quartos. In 1934 W.A. Jackson observed that 'Edward Gwynn is to the historians of English book collecting merely a name'[34] – well, he was certainly a name to Thomas Hearne as early as 1711.

I suspect that the 'certain Gentleman' who had noted Gwynn's books outside the Bodleian was John Bagford: it was certainly Bagford who put Hearne on to the significance of Humphrey Dyson's books in the library of Richard Smith. At the very time that Hearne was locked out of the Bodleian Library, he was noting the Dyson-Smith rarities in his diary. Once again, Hearne anticipated W.A. Jackson.[35]

Hearne's hunches about the rarity of books are well illustrated by the following note: 'Mr Rance [typesetter at the Sheldonian press] showed me a wonderfull small book printed at London by John Beale 1631, being intitled *The Book of Martyrs*. Tis an epitome of Fox, and the author was John Taylor (the Water-Poet, I thinke) and tis dedicated to the Rt. Hon. Phillip E. of Mountgomery. The Book is imperfect, one of the Parts being wanting.'[36] If you turn to *STC* 23732 you will find it listed as 64° in 16s, 'No copy traced . . . W.A. Jackson noted an unlocated fragment of Quire B from part 2 unfolded, with the above imprint, but attempts to trace it have failed.' Once again, Hearne was on the spot before W.A. Jackson.

Hearne was interested in the physical processes of printing. On page 1 of volume 50 of his diary he has pasted in Philippe de Galle's engraving of Stradanus's picture of an early printing press, and then gives a detailed analysis of the picture amounting to some 4000 words. You can compare it with Chapter V of part I of McKerrow's *Introduction to Bibliography* (1927), which analyses a number of pictures of early presses, and with F. Madan's article in *Bibliographica* (1895), which reproduces some of Hearne's comments.

A striking instance of Hearne's bibliographical expertise is his use of collation to establish priority of issue. In 1715 Thomas Bennet, a Colchester clergyman, published a book on the Thirty-Nine Articles. Bennet had discovered that there were important variations in Article 20 of the 1563 edition (see *STC* 10035 and Dr K. Pantzer's note), so his book contains an amazingly extensive bibliographical analysis of all the extant copies, in order to support his theological arguments. In an article in *The Library* (1951), 'Thomas Bennet, a forgotten bibliographer', Strickland Gibson drew attention to Bennet's book as a unique example of analytical bibliography in the early 18th century. But what Strickland Gibson did not mention was that the collations for all the copies available at Oxford were supplied by Thomas Hearne.[37] This omission is all the more remarkable because Hearne's correspondence with Bennet is easily accessible in the Bodleian, and the correspondence should have sent Gibson to the relevant parts of Hearne's diary.

Hearne's diaries provide us with ample evidence that Hearne was a classically trained textual editor who applied his mind to the whole range of 'modern' bibliographical problems. But there is one more illustration of Hearne's expertise: Hearne as a cataloguer.

Among the Library Records of the Bodleian Library you will find two volumes of Hearne's interleaved copy of Hyde's 1674 printed Bodleian catalogue and two further volumes of his projected supplement to Hyde.[38] It is very instructive to analyse Hearne's catalogue entries and to compare them with the entries in Robert Fysher's Bodleian catalogue of 1738 and with Bulkeley Bandinel's Bodleian catalogue of 1843.

Let us take two random examples:

A   Gabriel Biel, Spirensis: Vita & Expositio Canonis Missae, Lugd. 1542. 8°
Hearne: "NB *Versus Auctor* Expositionis Canonis Missae *sub Biel nomine editae* est
Eggeling, nescio quis, docente (ex ipsa prout videtur Bielii confessione) *Th. Raynaudo de
Mal. & Bon. lib.* p.140"
Fysher 1738: "[Eggeling, *nescio quis, Auctor hujusce Libri verus est*, v. Th. Raynaud, *de Mal. &
Bon. libb.* p.140]"
Bandinel 1843: "[Eggeling, nescio quis, auctor hujusce libri verus est. Conf. Th. Raynaud
de mal. & bon. libb.]"
B.   Georg. Erhardus: Symbolae in Petronium Arbitrum, una cum variorum com-
mentariorum sylloge, Hanov. 1621. 8°
Hearne: "Verus Auctor est Mich. Casp. Lundorpius, observante Placcio de Script. Anon.
& Pseudon. p.190"
Fysher 1738: "[Verus Auctor est Mich. Casp. Lundorpius, observante Placcio de Script.
Anon. & Pseud.]"
Bandinel 1843: "[verus auctor est Mich. Casp. LUNDORPIUS: v. Placcius de script. anon. &
pseud.]"

Hearne did not bother about fictitious imprints, but he did take the trouble to
try to get the correct attribution for the authors: and for that he used his own
extensive learning, coupled with the two available tools of his trade, M.J. Tho-
masius, *Disp. Philosophica de Plagio Literario*, Lips. 1673, 4° and V. Placcius *De
scriptoribus occultis detectis*, Hamb. 1674, 4° (he does not seem to have used the
second edition, Hamb. 1708). In the case of Gabriel Biel, he displays a knowledge
of Theophilus Raynaudus, *Erotemata de malis ac bonis libris*, Lugd. 1653, 4°, a work
unlikely to be in the *apparat* of many modern bibliographers. Hearne's general
legacy to the tradition of Bodleian cataloguing, after Hyde's catalogue of 1674,
was to make the Bodleian cataloguers more user-friendly, and to be generous
with cross-references and notes in their cataloguing entries. The expansive style
of entry in the 1738 and 1843 printed catalogues still has its value for bibliographers today. That tradition was continued in the old green laid-down manuscript
pre-1920 catalogues that were in general use in the Bodleian until very recently,
but which have now been replaced by *soi-disant* machine-readable ones.

After 1716, Hearne's Nonjuring principles caused him to be locked out of the
Bodleian, the library to which he had been devoted, and to which he had given the
best years of his life. Thereafter he used the Ashmolean and some of the college
libraries, and every few weeks his good friend Thomas Rawlinson would send
down from London a parcel of bibliographical rarities to keep up his spirits. But
Hearne had now to live entirely on the income derived from editing and publishing limited editions of English medieval chronicles, and most of his energy
went into that. On the open shelves of the Reading Room of the British Library
(at 2072 a. & b.) you will find nearly a dozen volumes of Hearne's medieval texts,
because they are still the best, or the only, editions that exist. They have been on
the open shelves of the Reading Room from its inception, and on the flyleaves
you will see Sir Hans Sloane's accession numbers: they were Sloane's subscription
copies, sent up to London by the carrier on the first day of issue from the
Sheldonian press – despite the fact that the ineffable Delegates of the Oxford Press
had done everything in their power to prevent their publication.

Conclusion

Wood's *Athenae* is a tangible bibliographical achievement: but even *that* needs saying and proving. Neither Bagford nor Hearne can be said to have left such enduring bibliographical monuments: but they do deserve attention as pioneers of bibliographical methodology – a methodology that was achieved solely by intellectual reflection on the materials before them, and without either financial subsidies or the aid of computers.

References

1. 1814 was also the year of publication of another landmark in the history of bibliography, T.H. Horne's *Introduction to the Study of Bibliography* (2 vols. Lond.).
2. A. Powell, *John Aubrey and his Friends*, Lond. 1948, p.127 *sq.*
3. The Bodleian *Summary Catalogue of Western Manuscripts*, Oxford 1895–1953, gives a full description of Wood's *nachlass*.
4. Bodley [MS] Wood E.13–22.
5. T. Bongaerts, *The Correspondence of Thomas Blount*, Amsterdam 1978, pp.31–33 and Bodley Wood 899(6 & 7).
6. The index to the Thomason Tracts was compiled by Bagford's friend, the bookseller Marmaduke Foster (cf. BL MS Harl.5911 f.42).
7. In *A National Library in Theory and Practice. The Panizzi Lectures 1987*. (British Library, 1988).
8. Wood, *Life and Times*, vol.III p.206.
9. BL MS Harl.5901 pt.I ff.24–32.
10. The previous occupant of 14 York Buildings was Samuel Pepys, so there is every reason to suppose that the Pepysian and the Harleian libraries had successively occupied the same room. Mr C.A. Rivington kindly drew my attention to Bagford's connection with Pepys. In Pepys's correspondence *circa* 1698 there is a note 'Bagford—send for', with a list of desiderata, and on 13 June 1700 Bagford and Wanley paid a visit to Pepys at Clapham (J.R. Tanner (ed.) *Private Correspondence . . . of Samuel Pepys*, Lond. 1926, vol.I pp.165, 166 & 360). Bagford supplied Pepys MS 2030.
11. BL MS Harl.5997 f.106 & 108. The printed Harleian catalogue wrongly gives his name as Flavill.
12. M.M. Gatch, 'John Bagford, Bookseller and Antiquary', *British Library Journal*, 12 (1986) pp.150–71, is a useful general summary.
13. BL MS Harl.5984.
14. BL MS Harl.5911 shows Bagford extracting bibliographical information from Ussher's letters, Beza's life of Calvin, and Strype's life of Parker; BL MS Sloane 923 f.20 shows the way he read Wood's *Athenae*, i.e. straight through.
15. Cf. BL MS Harl.5190 pt.IV f.241 *sq.*
16. M. Nickson 'Bagford and Sloane', *British Library Journal 9* (1983) pp.51–5, disposes of the myth concerning titlepages: Bateman the bookseller gave Bagford titlepages from imperfect copies which would otherwise have been disposed of as waste. BL MS Harl.5419 contains samples of manuscript transcripts of titlepages: there are many similar examples among the Bagford material in the BL Dept. of Printed Books.

17. *Cf.* BL MS Harl.5982 f.28.
18. C.L. Oastler, *John Day*, Oxf. 1975, p.1, pays a qualified tribute to Bagford's pioneering work on the biography of John Day.
19. *Cf.* BL MS Lansdowne 808 and Harl.5911 ff.104 & 106; and for Marprelate BL MS Harl.5910 pt.I f.8.
20. C. Davenport, 'Bagford's notes on Bookbindings', *Trans.Bibl. Soc.* 1904; E.G. Duff, *The Great Mearne Myth, Edinb. Bibl. Soc. XI* (1918); H.M. Nixon, *English Restoration Bookbindings*, Lond. 1974.
21. E.g. BL MS Harl.5910 pt.I f.239: notes of a rare volume of Scottish 'Sempill' tracts belonging to Anthony Wood, subsequently stolen from the Ashmolean library in the 19th century.
22. C.E. & R.C. Wright, *Diary of Humfrey Wanley*, Lond. 1966, vol.II p.451.
23. T.H. Aston (ed.), *History of the University of Oxford*, Oxf. 1986, vol.V pp.760–761.
24. H. Carter, *History of the Oxford University Press*, Oxf. 1975, vol.I pp.146–7 & 281. Hearne was elected Architypographus (at a salary ten times that of underkeeper of the Bodleian) by a vote of Convocation on 19 Jan. 1714–15. According to Carter: 'Always determined to be an oppressed man, after many acrimonious passages, he resigned the office on 7 November 1715.' Hearne had to refuse the post because, as a Nunjuror, his conscience forbad him to take the Oaths of Allegiance and Abjuration. It is a sad reflection on modern morality that a matter of conscience, involving grave financial loss, should be described as a determination to be an oppressed man. The way in which the Delegates of the Press censored and obstructed Hearne's publications is set out by Carter, rather too dispassionately, on pp.265–66. Enlightened liberal opinion seems to stop short at deploring press censorship when it is applied to Hearne. What is one to think of the Delegates of a university press who denied the Sheldonian imprint to an edition of Roper's life of Thomas More?
25. Hearne proudly presented a nicely bound copy to his patron Francis Cherry, the squire of Shottesbrooke. On Cherry's death it was acquired by Thomas Rawlinson. At the Rawlinson sales it was bought by Nicolas Berryer, a French Secretary of State who collected texts of Latin and Greek classics. Berryer's library was acquired in 1762 by Guillaume de Lamoignon, President of the Parlement of Paris, and at the Lamoignon sale in 1793 it was acquired by Mordaunt Cracherode, and so came to the British Museum in 1799: it is now BL 684.g.11.
26. *Remarks & Collections*, III p.233. This use of the word is not recorded in the *Oxford English Dictionary*.
27. *Remarks & Collections*, I p.95.
28. *Remarks & Collections,* I pp.101, 180, 104.
29. *Remarks & Collections*, I. p.177.
30. BL MS Harl. 5906 B f.69.
31. *Remarks & Collections*, II pp.194, 433, 442.
32. *Remarks & Collections*, II p.295.
33. *Remarks & Collections*, III p.171.
34. W.A. Jackson, *Records of a Bibliographer*, Cambridge, Mass., 1967, p.117.
35. *Remarks & Collections*, V pp.128–43, and Jackson *op.cit.* pp.135–41.
36. *Remarks & Collections*, III p.344.
37. *Remarks & Collections* IV p.157 etc.
38. Bodley MS Library Records c.1080–81 (Hearne's MS interleaved copy of 1674 cat.) and Library Records b.280–81 (MS supplement to 1674 cat.). These are discussed by

W.D. Macray, *Annals of the Bodleian Library*, Oxf. 1890, p.213. Hearne's quantitative contribution to the 1738 cat. is overstated, but he certainly imposed a clearly identifiable 'house style' on the 1738 cat. and thereby on the subsequent Bodleian cataloguing tradition.

Discussion following the paper

Contributors: Charles Rivington, Michael Harris, Keith Maslen.

Charles Rivington drew attention to Bagford's contacts with Pepys: Tom Birrell has incorporated this into the footnotes to his paper. Asked by Michael Harris about Philip Bliss's edition of the *Athenae Oxoniensis* Tom Birrell said that there were many projects for a revision of Wood and Bliss was able to work from Tanner's and Thomas Baker's annotated copies in the Bodleian. Bliss possessed the best collection of Wood material, and was very thorough and accurate.

A comment from Keith Maslen that Hearne was not too proud to hobnb with printers elicited the anecdote that Hearne was carried to his grave by his compositor, his engraver, his barber and his binder. He had virtually daily contact with his compositor. He was the only academic man in Oxford who had any practical knowledge about the day-to-day running of a press. In 1715 Convocation, which was dominated by Tories from Christ Church, elected Hearne to the post of Architypographus with the salary, which was large, of Superior Bedel of Civil Law. Nobody was better suited to be Architypographus than Hearne, but he was a Nonjuror and the moment he was made Superior Bedel the Delegates, who were all Whig, appointed the warehouseman, Stephen Richardson to act as Architypographus.

Stationers' Company Bibliographers: the first 150 years: Ames to Arber

ROBIN MYERS

'SOME OF THOSE persons treat folks as if they came as spies into their affairs,' Joseph Ames (1689–1759) grumbled to Maurice Johnson, founder of the Gentlemen's Society, Spalding. He wished he could 'get the same favour at Doctors' Commons and Stationers' Hall &c.'[1] as he got at the College of Heralds through the good offices of his friend John Anstis (1669–1744) who was Garter King of Arms from 1714. Ames was at work on a *Catalogue of Heads* which included portraits of early printers and he was also collecting material for the *Typographical Antiquities*, the first work to take serious account of the role of the Stationers' Company in the organisation and control of the 16th-century book trade.

'In my account of [typography's] most eminent men, I have added their privileges, licences, patents &c. which were granted to them,' he wrote in his preface, 'together with the names of their place, and sign at which they dwelt; the incouragements and discouragements they met with, as also the character of the Company of Stationers.' Yet Ames never came to Stationers' Hall, never saw the Entry Books of Copies and collected all his material elsewhere.

His friend and fellow Caxtonian, John Lewis[2] had tried to persuade him to write a much needed history of printing, but he had heard that the printer Samuel Palmer (d1732) was engaged on just such a project and Ames 'thought himself by no means equal to an undertaking of so much extent.'[3] When Palmer died with only the technical part of his work completed George Psalmanazar[4] was commissioned to ghost the rest. When the *General History of Printing* came out in 1732 'it by no means answered the expectations of Mr Lewis or Mr Ames, or those of the publick in general'[5] and Ames was persuaded to set to work and fill the gap himself. He spent the next 17 years in 'collecting and arranging his materials' both historical and graphic. He had 'very early discovered a taste for English history'[6] and, as first secretary of the recently founded Society of Antiquaries his circle (though his living came from trading as an ironmonger and ship's chandler in Wapping) included bibliophiles and antiquaries who 'largely assisted him' as he said, with advice and the use of the books in their libraries. Edward Rowe Mores, with the condescension of the cléric for the man of trade and autodidact, dismissed Ames as 'unlearned ... but useful,'[7] but he worked systematically from the best sources available to him.

'I did not chuse to copy into my book from catalogues,' he wrote in the preface, 'but from the books themselves, and have added a very copious Index of persons' names who are mentioned, by using of which anything in the book may be found.' In addition to 'books themselves', he worked from a copy of Maunsell's *Catalogue of English Printed Books on Divinity*, 1595, which he annotated heavily. It later came into the hands of William Herbert who further annotated it. After Herbert's death Arrowsmith and Bowley auctioned it in a sale of the third part of Herbert's library in November 1798. It is now in the Huntington Library, California. As well as using many books belonging to himself and to friends, title pages separated from books also provided Ames with many imprint details. He amassed a vast collection of 'old title pages and heads of authors which he tore out and maimed books.'[8] Biblioclast we may call him, and William Blades[9] would certainly have done so had he realised how much Ames had sinned; but then Rowe Mores excused him; 'he was but one sinner among many.'[10] The works of Stow, Dugdale and the indefatigable Strype were also the source of much of his material.

That none of his data came from Stationers' Hall is the conclusion I have come to after close scrutiny of numerous entries on individual stationers in the *Antiquities* as well as the general history section. Nor is Ames mentioned in the court orders, although that does not provide proof positive of his not coming to the hall, for we find later researchers often came more times than is recorded in the court books. As a City man (he was bound to a plane-maker who was free of the Joiners' Company) and although it is doubtful if he was ever freed he would have had easy access to the Chamberlain's register of Freemen and lists of journeymen's licences, which were open to merchants' inspection at a time when City trading was restricted to Freemen and City dwellers. He could have found the names of early printers in the registers and obtained some of the data concerning their 'privileges, licences, patents &c. which were granted to them.' Among other repositories that he searched was the Prerogative Office where, 'by favour of Mr Legard'[11] he saw Robert Redman's will.

In the section on the general history of printing Ames gives a transcript in English of the Stationers' Company's first, royal charter of 1557. There are two extant English translations of this; the earlier is contained in a manuscript volume at Stationers' Hall of 'all the Company's grants relating to the corporation and English Stock with translations of such as are in Latin'. This is not the one Ames used but that 'translated from the original Latin by Henry Rooke which agrees with the Record now remaining in the Chapel of the Rolls, and . . . examined by me this 8th Day of December, 1741.' Rooke (or Rook), as a friend of Ames' and a fellow bibliophile might have let Ames see his translation; or he might have used a copy of the *Charters and grants of the Company of Stationers . . .* printed by Richard Nutt, 1741. Nutt had produced and circulated this pamphlet among the Company's Yeomanry in an attempt to rouse them to rebellion against the court, forcing them 'to redress the Hardships and Miseries of the injured and oppressed Freemen'. I do not known how many were printed, nor whether it circulated outside the Company. It is not included in Langford's sale catalogue of Ames's library in May 1760, which seems to suggest that he did not ever own a copy.

Rooke may also have procured transcriptions of the various patents and privileges granted to individual stationers which Ames prints in the general history. There are none, in any case, at Stationers' Hall.

The first part of the *Antiquities* is a pioneer biographical dictionary of printers with each entry appended by a list, in date order as far as possible, of works each had printed. The second part, a seminal history of printing in London, the provinces, Scotland and Ireland, provided an overview. His purpose was largely bibliophilic: 'Gentlemen may be assisted to complete their antient books which often are imperfect at the beginning, or end, by copying from this'.[12]

'One test of a really good and useful book,' Henry Bradshaw wrote to the Royal Librarian at the Hague in 1874 'is that it should enable you at once to rise beyond it and bring a number of facts to light – that it should afford the means of correcting its own mistakes.'[13] Ames's *Typographical Antiquities* is one such 'good and useful book' and Ames set to work as soon as it was published to annotate an interleaved copy, perhaps with the intention of bringing out a revised edition in due course. At the Langford sale, 'Ames's History of Printing with the addition of some 100 articles in MSS . . . Copper Plates, blocks and copy-right of the same book', the annotated Maunsell catalogue, two copies of the Stationers' 1678 Orders, Rules and Ordinances, the 1637 Star Chamber Decree and 'another sixteen 17th century printing items'[14] (not identified) were all bought by Sir Peter Thompson (1698–1770), Ames's friend, fellow merchant and collector, who later sold all or most of them to William Herbert.

Herbert (1718–95), a native of Hitchin, was bound to a City hosier and after being freed he set up as a hosier in Leadenhall Street before turning to glass painting. After a spell as a ship's purser for the East India Company and an adventurous sojourn in India, he returned to City trading as a print-seller and engraver of charts, first on old London Bridge and then, after the bridge houses were pulled down in 1756–8, in Goulston Square, Leadenhall Street, not far from his first shop. Increasing popularity and, we may suppose, the increased contact with the book trade which his last occupation afforded him, gave him the means of accumulating a large library. A late and much married man, he increased his affluence yet further by his three marriages to widows or single ladies with jointures. Soon after burying his second wife he 'ventured,' in John Nichols's words,[15] the third time, on a match with a lady whom he used to visit in Goulston Square as a neighbour'. In 1769 he 'succeeded to his utmost wishes as a vendor of charts and prints, and resolved to retire equally from business and the metropolis; and with this view, purchased a country residence at Cheshunt in Hertfordshire . . . his favourite room being the library . . . and there he used to sit, under a circular skylight, in the intervening period of every meal . . . and he always flew from his eating room to his library'.

'The increasing taste for the specimens of our first printers, and the great discoveries which it produced, first suggested to me the idea of continuing Mr Ames's labours,' he explained in the preface to his revision of the *Antiquities*. Having possessed himself of Ames's interleaved copy of this work with Ames's notes, the copyright and plates, he 'thought there could not be offered a more acceptable present to the lovers of science than a republication of this work with the author's own improvements, and what further could be collected from my own observations and those of my learned friends'.

'His diligence . . . was amazing,' wrote Dibdin. 'His application to possess himself of every article of information, that libraries or auctions could furnish him with, was intense. The incouragement he received from the collectors of black-leather books, from His Majesty's library to the smallest library of an individual, he has gratefully acknowledged in his preface.'[16] He acknowledges some 50 persons who put their books at his disposal, or who otherwise helped him with his research over the 25 years that he spent preparing the first two volumes of his revision of the *Antiquities*. Several of the repositories which were closed to Ames opened their doors to Herbert through his personal contacts. At Guildhall, to which it was notoriously difficult to gain access, his friend Henry Parker examined some of the records for him. Parker (*d.*1809) was a fellow print-seller who had bought the lucrative post of Clerk to the Chamber at Guildhall on retiring from trade in 1774. He was Master of the Stationers' Company (1801–2) and presented the Company with an engraved portrait of Tycho Wing the almanack maker. 'His remarkable placidity of . . . manners very much endeared him to a circle of sincere friends',[17] Herbert being one. Another useful friend acknowledged in the preface was Thomas Astle (1735–1803), antiquary and palaeographer, who was Royal Commissioner for methodising the state papers at Whitehall (1764) and then Chief Clerk, and later Keeper of the Record Office in the Tower. From him Herbert obtained details of documents in the paper-office and the Tower.

Herbert had expected that a two-volume edition 'might comprize all the additional materials' but no sooner had he circulated a proposal in 1780 than 'a respectable friend' suggested that 'my book would be very defective unless i procured the entries of copies licensed by the master and wardens of the Stationers' Company'.[18] Accordingly, and without realising what he was embarking on, he applied to his friend, the learned bookseller, Lockyer Davis (1718–91), Immediate Past Master of the Stationers' Company, and 'by his kind intercession . . . leave was granted me to have the use of their Register Books'. The court of 4 July 1780 ordered 'that Mr William Herbert of Cheshunt in the County of Hertford do have the use of the severall Books of Entries belonging to this Company, one at a time, giving receipts for the same respectively, with a promise to return them upon Demand'.[19] It may seem strange that Herbert was allowed to take away and use without supervision, the earliest and most precious record books when Ames only 40 years earlier had been denied access to Stationers' Hall; but the climate of the trade had changed in the intervening years. When Ames applied to the Hall, the Company's control of the trade through the operation of the Licensing laws was still within living memory; by Herbert's day that was history. Even so, the Stationers' Company continued to be a rather secretive body for a long time to come and to 'treat folks as if they came as spies into their affairs' unless they had a member of the court or some other important member of the Company to intercede for them.

Herbert must have returned Register A before 28 September when the court ordered that it be lent to Mr Wharton of Oxford.[20] Although Herbert is only mentioned once in the court orders we know that he borrowed Register A again, as well as Liber B and after 1790, when volume III of the *Antiquities* was published, he used Liber C and came to the Hall.

Like Ames before him, he continued to work on the *Antiquities* to the end of his life. In addition to annotating Ames's copy, he had his own edition interleaved which extended it to six volumes. After Herbert's death it passed to Richard Gough and in 1810 Dibdin bought it at the Gough Sale. Dibdin removed a number of the interleaves and text with Herbert's marginalia from the first three volumes. He later sold it to Lennox who offered it to the British Museum in exchange for a duplicate *Soutos Relacam* and an imperfect Hakluyt *Voyages*, 1582, in March 1849. 'Upon Mr Panizzi's recommendation the Trustees sanction[ed] the exchange...proposed'. Copies of the letters suggesting and authorising the exchange are tipped into this interleaved set, which was kept behind the door of the Keeper's office in the British Museum and 'was redeemed from this rather ignominious position as late as May 1977 and given a shelf mark'.[21]

The margins are crammed with new material collected after publication of Volume III, including the names of benefactors of the Stationers' Company on a list 'set up in the Dineing Room of Ye Stationers' Company,' which has long since disappeared. In the margin of the article relating to each benefactor he notes his place in the list; against that on William Norton, for example, he writes: 'stands second in the list of benefactors...'.[22]

A marginal comment next to the entry on the title page of *England's Parnassus* notes that he had been unable to identify the printer before publication 'Mr Mason's copy and mine giving only the initial letters, and not having seen the Stationers' Register C at the time the sheet was printed...'.[23]

Herbert transcribed Register A, Liber B and selections from Liber C into three quarto notebooks which together total some 900 pages. He had them bound in vellum lined with map waste (no doubt leftovers from his chart engraving days) and labelled 'Entries of Copies &c. at Stationers' Hall' with volume number and dates covered by each. Samuel Bentley is disparaging in his Index to the *Literary Anecdotes* of the 'unhandsome copy of the Register's'[24] but to our latter-day eyes they are quite otherwise; they are legible and serviceable even after 200 years of damp and biting of the gall in the ink into the paper in many places.

The third notebook is somewhat different from the other two; it consists of two wrapped notebooks containing Liber C transcriptions, 7 July 1598 to 12 November 1608, covering the same years as the Maunsell catalogue which Herbert had already annotated extensively. Moreover Herbert, being now in his seventies, may have felt time running out on him and thought to shorten the labour of transcription by omitting duplicated entries. Two further booklets bound into notebook C consist of a transcription and commentary on the Decrees and Ordinances 1576 to 1602 'concerning printing and copy-right...extracted from...Hall Book Letter B'. It is ironic that Herbert was allowed to make use of those very ordinances which the court considered too confidential for Arber to publish nearly a hundred years later. Yet the Clerk, Charles Rivington, in his exhaustive report on the records in 1842 saw no harm in Herbert's work, conscious though he was of the dignity of the Company: 'though rebuked by Mr Nichols in the Literary Anecdotes for the excessive use of the privilege granted to him to inspect the Company's books . . . yet he does not appear to have published anything detrimental to the interests of the Company,'[25] he wrote. Search as I may through the *Anecdotes* I can find no such stricture.

'Whatever pressure Herbert may have felt while the press waited for him to complete his work, the transcript is reliable within its limitations;' wrote Franklin Dickey, '. . . whatever he records he sets down with considerable though not absolute accuracy, his infrequent slips being caused by ignorance or by misreading, faults of which Arber is not entirely free . . . there are possibly a few more errors in the transcript of the neat and regular Register A than in that of the much more demanding Liber B.'[26] Herbert consistently used his own abbreviations for the introductory formulae of the entries. He used the same code in the annotations of the *Antiquities* where he was scrupulous in differentiating, by the use of an asterisk, 'those articles which were Ames's own and those which have no owner assigned to them and rest on the authority of collections made at sales, &c. and often from Maunsell'.[27]

It was use of the Stationers' entry books, more than any other single source, that enabled Herbert to rise above Ames's 'good and useful book', as comparison of the two editions shews. Ames, for example, gives three quarters of a page to William Norton (1527–93), printer of the Bishop's Bible (1595) and benefactor of the company's loan bequest named after him. Ames cites Stow as his source and copies from him the biographical epitaph which Dugdale transcribed from Norton's tomb for his History of St Paul's. Ames lists five books which Norton printed.[28] Herbert, in contrast, gives five pages to Norton, lists 25 books entered to him in the register, two of which he notes were entered jointly with other men, as well as listing other books which Norton had licenses for. He takes from Liber B the dates of Norton's clothing, service as Renter, Under and Upper Warden, a fine for misdemeanour and details of his will.[29]

The last stationer in the dictionary section is Simon Stafford or Strafford. Ames's article comprises, merely, his place of publication 'on Addle Hill, near Carter Lane' and a list of four books published 1599 to 1603.[30] With the aid of Liber B, Herbert lists 10 books entered to Stafford, gives an account of his infringement, with William Barley, of the privilege for grammars and accidences, the dates of his arrest, seizure of his press, being refused the Company's Freedom, and how 'the 7 May following, to prevent further litigation, he was translated from the Drapers; and being made free of the Stationers' Company, then unmolested he printed the following books . . . '. He adds a footnote transcription of the Order in Council, copied in full from Liber B.[31] Plomer's entry, though fuller, is largely derived from Herbert.[32]

Herbert added little to the general history section of the *Antiquities*, but, in the preface and elsewhere there are some penetrating observations on the workings of the 16th-century trade; he was undoubtedly the first to realise that the booksellers separated from the printers very early and soon came to dominate the Company. 'Towards the end of Queen Elizabeth's reign [the booksellers] became the sole publishers of books, employing [the printers] to print for them as at this day . . . many of the articles entered in the Stationers' Registers would have been unnoticed, had not separate accounts been made for those who were booksellers or stationers, but not printers. Indeed, the booksellers appear to have been altogether denominated stationers at that time.'[33]

Collectors and collecting stamped 18th-century bibliographical practice and both Ames and Herbert regarded their histories as serving those 'lovers of science' with a 'taste for specimens of our first printers' who were eager to learn all they could about the background of the books in the libraries. Nor was Herbert ignorant of the fashionable field of Shakespeariana which was attracting some of the best scholars of the day as well as the romantic bardoloters, and even the downright reprehensible, I mean the Shakespeare forgers. George Steevens (1736–1800) was a friend whose work and whose library Herbert knew well: 'See Mr Steevens letter to me', 'George Steevens Esq has a copy of verse in Manuscript entitled A Description of the World', 'I am informed by my good friend, George Steevens Esq. who possesses this very scarce book. W.H.' are some of the comments to be found in the text or annotations of Herbert's *Antiquities*. He also knew the work of Steevens's one time protegé Edmond Malone: 'The whole is reprinted in Malone's supplement to ye edition of Shakespeare's plays published 1778,'[34] is written in the margin beside the article on Tottel's *Tragicall Hystory of Romeus and Juliet*, 1562. There, for the time being let us leave Herbert, 'early in the morning before breakfast in the centre of his library under the skylight window' wearing 'a white, formally curled wig – to which was frequently superadded a white hat'.[35]

George Steevens, third in our story, was probably the first to gain admittance to Stationers' Hall, although Arber, in his survey of early researchers, thought otherwise. He must surely be Herbert's 'respectable friend' who advised him that the revision of the *Antiquities* would be 'very defective' unless he made use of the Hall registers. Steevens was engaged by Dr Johnson to revise his edition of Shakespeare; Boswell described him as 'a gentleman not only deeply skilled in ancient learning, and of very extensive reading in English literature, especially the early writers, but at the same time of acute discernment and elegant taste.'[36] Johnson gave him an introduction to Dr Farmer at Cambridge, whose essay on the learning of Shakespeare started a considerable vogue. 'He is a very ingenious gentleman,' Johnson commended him to Farmer,'. . . who has collected an account of all the translations which Shakespeare might have seen and used.'[37] Steevens included a 'List of ancient translations from Classick Authors' in his second revision of 1778.

Steevens was certainly at work on the Stationers' Registers in 1774 because he wrote in the margin of the Shakespeare entry of f.193 of Liber B his starred initials and the date, 'G*S 1774'. 'He did not scruple to put his initials against every entry that interested him,' wrote John Payne Collier[38] and Herbert copied them into his notebooks and annotated *Antiquities*. Franklin Dickey is inclined to condone what 'was never meant to deceive' but I, as curator of the records, do not take such a lenient view. No doubt these marginal 'G*S' were pointers easing an arduous task; 'by far the most irksome part of my undertaking,' Steevens commented, 'though facilitated, as much as possible, by the Kindness of Mr Longman, of Paternoster Row, who readily furnished me with the three volumes of the records of the Stationers-Company, together with the accommodation which rendered the perusal of them convenient to me, though troublesome to himself.'[39] It is difficult to think what this troublesome accommodation could be, but it is the word used again in the court order of 7 February 1797 giving permission to 'Mr George Steevens Esq. to inspect the entry books and every necessary accommodation be provided for him during such inspection.'[40] Thomas Longman (1730–97) nephew of the founding Longman, succeeded to the business in 1755 and was a man of sufficient consequence, although he was not called on to court until 1778, to get Steevens past the guarded portals. Steevens used the entry books extensively, as a comparison of the two Johnson-Steevens editions of 1773 and 1778 shews. The lists of 'ancient editions of Shakspere's plays', of 'plays ascribed to Shakspere', and of 'ancient translations from classick authors' are all full of references to entry. 'Mr Steevens remarks on entries of the Stationers-Company' emphasises, at some length, the importance of the entry books as a source for dating Shakespeare's plays; with the euphoria of those who break new ground he asserts 'The public is now in possession of as accurate an account of the dates &c. of Shakespeare's works, as perhaps will ever be compiled.'[41] Edmond Malone who was his protégé at that time had made an 'attempt to ascertain the Order in which the Plays . . . were written', basing much of his evidence on Steevens's work on the entry books. Steevens acknowledges Malone's 'Chronology' handsomely: 'By the aid of the registers at Stationers-Hall, and such internal evidence as the pieces themselves supply Mr Malone has so happily accomplished his undertaking, that he only leaves me the power to thank him for an arrangement which I profess my inability either to dispute or to improve.'[42] Malone, who had settled in London only the year before, soon began to outstrip his mentor and by 1785 the friendship was destroyed by Malone's outspoken criticism of Steevens's notes to the 1778 edition. Malone never considered feelings when in pursuit of intellectual truth and Steevens was, in any case, always quick to take offence.

Malone is mentioned in the court orders three times, in November 1789, February 1790 and July 1800,[43] but he may well have come earlier. On the first two occasions he was permitted to borrow Liber B 'on his giving a Receipt for the same, with a Promise to return it'. When he sought to use all three volumes for the third time, 'it was ordered that the Books be left with the Treasurer for Mr Malone's inspection, but that they are not to be taken from the hall'. Shall we deduce that the new clerk, Henry Rivington, the first of the clerkly Rivington dynasty, exercised tighter control than his predecessor, the easy-going Joseph Baldwin (clerk, 1776–1800)? It is also possible that they were on the trail of the starred 'G*S' because when John Nichols asked leave for Alexander Chalmers to inspect the early entry books in 1802, it was granted 'upon the express condition that no books shall be removed from the Hall, nor any Mark or Writing whatever be made in them.'[44] Infer from that what you will! Malone used the entry books a great deal in preparation for his edition of Shakespeare, (1790–6) and sought to improve on his first attempt at a chronology of Shakespeare's plays. Chronology, indeed became something of a battle cry. Foraging in the entry books was heady wine to serious scholars and 'bardolaters' alike, which, together with the records of the Master of the Revels seemed capable of solving any Shakespearean enigma. In the battle of the books which raged over the Ireland forgeries of 1795–6 the entry books were used as weapons of attack and defence by Steevens and Malone on the one side and George Chalmers on the other. Because W.H. Ireland soon confessed the fraud and 'exposure'[45] was pointless, Malone's onslaught was directed less at the Irelands, father and son, than at those experts who had been deceived in the first place. He brought the weight of his forensic skill to his *Inquiry into the Authenticity of Certain Miscellaneous Papers... Attributed to Shakespeare* in 431 well researched and scathing pages – which brings us to the fifth, the least known but one of the most important early users of the Hall records.

George Chalmers (1742–1825), who had been one of those gulled by the forgeries, was nettled at the aspersions which Malone and Steevens cast on his learning and acumen, and he defended his position in two lengthy apologies, 1797 and 1799. Two would seem an excessive number but scholars are now realising that the *Supplemental Apology for the Believers in the Shakespeare-Papers... 1799* stands, as Arthur Freeman puts it, 'among his most estimable achievements... if his contribution to scholarly method is ever to be reassessed.'[46] Sam Schoenbaum adds that 'Chalmers makes a contribution of his own to Elizabethan studies in his discussion [among other things] of the Shakespeare chronology.'[47] Late in the autumn of 1798 Chalmers approached the bookseller William Chapman, Past Master of the Stationers' Company, to ask him to seek permission to work on Liber B and C. Accordingly, the court of 6 November ordered that 'George Chalmers Esq. have liberty to inspect at the Hall the Books of Entries for the years 1576 to 1599.'[48] It was at this point that two of the Herbert notebooks came on the market. Herbert had died in January 1796 and his library was sold in three parts. The first was auctioned by Leigh and Sotheby in March; a further 2700 volumes went to his bookseller nephew, Isaac Herbert, who sold them from a catalogue 'on reasonable terms for Ready Money, at the prices printed in the Catalogue' which included Ames's annotated copy of the *Antiquities*. The rest of Herbert's books were auctioned by Arrowsmith and Bowley 21 to 25 November 1798 when Chalmers, a fortnight after applying for leave to use the entry books, bought lot 961 for 16 guineas. This was described as 'Stationers' Company Register Books, A and B, copies from the Originals, in the Company's Hall, by Mr Herbert.' Later, but I do not know where or when, Chalmers also acquired the third Herbert notebook, all three having his spade shield book plate pasted over or next to Herbert's anonymous Jacobean one. Whether the Herbert notebooks led Chalmers to Stationers' Hall or the other way round I have no means of knowing at present; but I have a great deal more work to do on Chalmers's association with the Stationers' records, having recently learnt that the manuscript of his unpublished history of Scottish printing is in the National Library of Scotland, which may or may not yield some more clues.

The later history of the Herbert notebooks is linked to another strand of Stationers' Company scholarship, that of the history of the Company itself. It can only be touched on here for the light it sheds on early use of the records. In his report on the Company's archives and their use by scholars, already quoted from, the clerk, Charles Rivington offered himself as Company historian. John Nichols had already published a 200-page article in the *Literary Anecdotes*, vol.III, which drew on the Herbert notebooks; but the time was thought ripe for an official history sponsored by the Company itself.

'It would need much discrimination and judgement . . . with reference to the interests of the Corporation and English Stock,' the clerk argued, 'in printing what when once given to the public can never be recalled; and that if undertaken by a stranger . . . would require strict superintendence on the part of the Court . . . ' (as Edward Arber found to his cost some 30 years later). The project was still-born, but in preparing for it the Company bought the Herbert notebooks when Chalmers's library was sold that same year (1842). He had died in 1825. C.R. Rivington succeeded his father as clerk on the latter's death in 1869 and took over the task of producing a seemly history which would not be 'injurious to the interests or derogatory to the dignity of the Company.'[50] He read it to the Company in 1881 and it was printed in expanded form in 1883. It contains the lists of Royal, Oxford, Cambridge and City of London printers taken verbatim from Herbert's notebook C, without acknowledgement, and there are other signs that Rivington drew heavily on Herbert. Not the least of these is the subsequent provenance of notebook C which got separated from its fellows once more, mixed up with Rivington's private books and 'inadvertently sold at his death in 1928'.[51] Some time later W.A. Jackson was book-hunting in Cambridge and came across it, marked three guineas, in Galloway and Porter's shop in Sidney Street. He bought it, made use of it while at work on his edition of court book C, and then generously gave it back to the Company where it rejoined its fellows in the muniment room. It now has Galloway's bookseller's ticket as well as the bookplates of Herbert, Chalmers and Jackson.

Chalmers used the Herbert notebooks when he was at work on Liber B and C; he added some pertinent comments, a few corrections and put pencil crosses against certain entries. Herbert had also used pencil here and there, though more frequently ink, now sepia with age. In any case his flowing mid-Georgian hand is easily distinguished from Chalmers's small, neat notes in a later hand and darker brown ink, and he did not use red at all, as Herbert did for some annotations. Chalmers put his pencil crosses against the Scottish printers, and many more against those Shakespeare entries which were the basis for his notes in three sections of the *Supplemental Apology*[53] which is an important addition to Shakespeare scholarship because, in it, Chalmers makes use of the entry books in a new way. The section on Shakespeare's 'note of hand' uses the Wardens' Accounts to exemplify, for the first time the financial and political operation of the City Companies. Chalmers's methodology is important and is not invalidated by the fact that the Ireland forgeries are too blatantly spurious to be credible to us. Yet the analogy with City accounting stands: 'It was an adequate Apology for the Believers,' Chalmers maintains, 'that they produced similar documents, in the same age, by whatever denomination they were known, whether by that of bill or note...'. He instances 'specimens of similar documents, which I found on the Registers of the Stationers' Company,' one being 'Bonham Norton's promise to pay 20s' a fine for non-service as underwarden 'within one yere next; and further, iff his XXId lent to her Majesties in this Court shall be repaid before the end of the said yere, it shall go presently upon the receipt thereof to the satisfaction of the said fine, of XXId...'.[54]

Chalmers also identifies 31 plays licensed by the Master of the Revels, Sir George Bucke, 'as appears by the Stationers. These dates,' he adds, 'correct what was said, on this subject, in the *Apology*.'

Chalmers' emendations of Herbert's 'good and useful' notebooks shew how they 'afforded the means of correcting their own mistakes'. One such is the memo Chalmers added to Herbert's transcription of the entry of Nashe's *Lenten Stuff* in notebook A: 'It is absolutely impossible that the "Nashe's Lenten Stuffe" here entered by W. Pickering, can mean (as Mr Herbert supposes) Nashe's tract with that title, which was not published until 1599. Nashe was a child in 1570.'[55]

Herbert believed that the *Clerk's book* had gone astray and ends notebook A with a memo on p.253 to that effect: 'I leave the residue of this book for inserting extracts from the Clerk's Book (not found)'. He may be referring to the lost 'white book or clerk's book of printed books deposited' which once existed. He also refers several times to a 'Register in Ye Clerk's Book (not found)', but Chalmers, following the lead of Steevens and Malone, believes that that particular clerk's book was what we now called Register A, the earliest surviving volume of records, which Steevens reported lost and Malone subsequently found. Chalmers commented in the *Supplemental Apology*: 'The fact is, as Mr Greenhill the Company's Treasurer assured me, this volume was never lost; But, it was only not recognised, at the time, being without the distinguishing mark of A, on the back; nor, has it any mark upon its cover, to this day'.[56] This certainly sounds suspiciously like Register A which has not 'any mark upon its cover' except for a paper label 'Wordens' Acounts' on the spine, now collapsed, and even more easily overlooked than it was in Chalmers's day. Finally, the Herbert notebooks, which run like a thread through early use of the Stationers' entry books, served to uncover the Collier forgeries in Liber B long after both Herbert and Collier were gone to dust.

John Payne Collier (1789–1883), the last of the early users, was, in the words of Sam Schoenbaum, 'one of the most eminent Shakespeare editors of the 19th century in the period between the death of Edmond Malone in 1813 and the rise of the "new bibliography".'[57] It is unfortunate that he was tempted during much of his long life to make additions to certain primary documents to which he gained access to and which lacked the data he would have liked them to have. He was no callow W.H. Ireland producing puerile forged documents in order to curry favour with a father besotted with bardolotry, but an astute scholar-forger who could not rest content with the considerable reputation he had gained on the level. So skilful was he that it was not until 1960 that his tamperings with the Stationers' entry book, 'though for some time scholars had privately suspected'[58] as much, were finally proved beyond all doubt.

It was well-known that his 'Extracts from the Registers . . . 1557–95', published by the Shakespeare Society in 1848 and '49, and in Notes and Queries, 1861 and '63, were not all they purported to be. On 7 December 1847 the court ordered that 'Mr John Payne Collier and Mr Halliwell be permitted to inspect the Registers of Copies in the reigns of Elizabeth and James I.' It was the first of many visits, though the only one mentioned in the court books. Collier himself thanked the Master, Wardens and Court most fulsomely in his introduction for 'the facilities liberally afforded to him.'[59] Franklin Dickey believes that it was only on this first occasion that Halliwell accompanied him; book thief though Halliwell was, he can be exonerated from the charge of forger since 'he turned one of Collier's most indignant critics when other forgeries were discovered.'[60] Collier's sponsor in the Company was the youthful Joshua Butterworth, 30 years old, who was not called on court until 1889, and was Master (1894–5). Collier seems to have been given a free run by charming and bambozzling all at Stationers' Hall. The old Treasurer George Greenhill and his son, assistant and successor Joseph were 'returned effusive thanks . . . for most ready and patient assistance . . .'.[61]

Like all forgers Collier left plenty of clues, including, Franklin Dickey found, 'scattered remarks . . . throughout his critical writings'. There are several such for those whose eyes have once been opened, in the preface to the 1848 Extracts . . . with Notes and Illustrations 1557 to 1570.

'Nothing,' Collier declared in the preface, 'can prove more decisively the vast abundance of such once-existing materials than the volume now in the hands of the Shakespeare Society . . . ' Collier was quarrying Liber B not for Shakespeare entries, but for the 'hundreds of ballads and broadsides, to say nothing of tracts and chapbooks, [which] have been lost, all of them interesting, with a view to the state of opinions, feelings, manners, and customs, among the great body of the nation'.

Collier was unwise, though, posthumously, to take the name of the 'industrious and learned' Herbert in vain, as he did in the preface, for 'constantly dismiss[ing] his account of an early printer by the general and most disappointing intelligence, that, besides the works . . . enumerated . . . he published "many ballads and broadsides" the titles and subjects of which are not even hinted at'. Thereupon Collier set to work to repair Herbert's omission with ballads of his own composition purporting to be by Elizabethan ballad makers 'on themes suggested by entries in the Registers'. And quite good ballads they are, when all is said and done, though fraudulent. Collier then turned his attention to Liber B again and added those names of authors so strangely omitted by the clerk or beadle entering 18, or possibly 19 of these ephemeral works. Arber transcribed all the added names as genuine although he spotted Steevens's 'G*S' as later adornments and left them out. His opinion of those who had worked on the records shews how completely he fell into Collier's trap: 'STEEVENS, MALONE,

DOUCE, CHALMERS, RITSON made use of [the registers] for special purposes; but it was the most excellent endeavour of Mr JOHN PAYNE COLLIER to cull such Book Entries as related to the Drama and Popular Literature &c. &c. down to... 1595.'62

Franklin Dickey, with the help of Cyprian Blagden, and the check that Herbert's notebook C provides by antedating Collier's transcripts by some 60 years, finally nailed the forgeries; for Herbert's notebook is, of course, without the tell-tale addition of authors of anonymous ballads. The unlikelihood of authors' names being subsequently inserted for ephemeral works originally entered anonymously provides circumstantial evidence; no author entered 'for his copy' until after the Queen Anne statute of 1710 and it was of no consequence to the 16th-century wardens of the Company, or to the entering bookseller or printer who an author was when no financial interest was at stake. So no clerk or beadle would be likely to inscribe a missing author's name 'either in the left hand margin where the copy owner's name is entered, or [to squeeze] it in beneath the entry, or clumsily [to insert] it in the space left... between the end of the entry and the record of payment for entry'. The handwriting provides yet further evidence of forgery. Dickey found that 'by studying the Collier forgeries... we can determine the unvarying characteristics of Collier's imitation of secretary hand... There are purely calligraphic qualities which identify the forgeries for a suspicious investigator, which the generous Arber was not... [but] there is nothing improbable about the handwriting itself.'62 No doubt forensic evidence, which I hope to obtain in due course, will make assurance doubly sure.

Collier's 'unrestricted use' of Liber B brings us to the end of the first wave of Stationers' Company bibliographers who limited their researches to the three earliest books, now known as Register A, Liber B and Liber C covering the years 1556–1620. Those outside the Company consulted them for a few circumscribed purposes, either as bibliophiles verifying facts about the first printers, or seeking to establish the Shakespeare canon and chronology, or unearthing titles of old popular literature for antiquarian researches. These first bibliographers transcribed and published very small sections of the records; those few inside the Company itself – the Nicholses and the Rivingtons – proudly produced what were little more than house histories, useful in their way but carefully suppressing or interpreting what they felt might shew the Company which they were so proud of in a damaging light. Edward Arber (1836–1912) wove all the strands of the early bibliographers together when, officially backed by the Company though with misgivings and restrictions, he published his monumental *Transcript of the registers... 1554–1640*. This heralded the 'new bibliography' of Pollard, Greg, Plomer and others by giving scholars access to a large enough amount of the early records to enable them to work at a distance from Stationers' Hall.

Sources (In the order that they occur in the text)

Joseph Ames. *Typographical Antiquities*, 1749 (cited as *Ames*). Interleaved, bound in 3 vols. and annotated by Ames, and later by Herbert, and minimally by Dibdin, now in the British library (cited as *annotated Ames*).
Revised edition by William Herbert, 3 vols. 1785, 1786, 1790. Interleaved, bound in 6 vols, annotated by Herbert, and minimally by Dibdin, now in the British Library (cited as *annotated Herbert*). Another edition, with mainly anecdotal notes, by Thomas Frognal Dibdin, 4 vols. 1810. (Cited as Dibdin.)

William Herbert. *Book of entries at Stationers' Hall A 1571–1576*. MS transcript with additional notes by Herbert and George Chalmers (cited as *Herbert notebook A*).
Ditto from 7 July 1598 to 4 July 1603. B (cited as *Herbert notebook B*).
Ditto C (1598 to 1620 (cited as *Herbert notebook C*).

Andrew Maunsell. *Catalogue of English printed books on divinity*, 1595, annotated by Ames & Herbert (cited as *annotated Maunsell*).

John Nichols. *Literary ancedotes of the eighteenth century*, 9 vols. 1812 (cited as *L.A.*).

Samuel Palmer. *General History of Printing*, 1732 (cited as *Palmer*).

George Steevens. 2nd revised edition of Johnson's Shakespeare. 10 vols. 1778 (cited as *Steevens*).
Prolegomena to the dramatick writings of Will. Shakspere. 1788. This is the prefatory material to Steevens-Johnson's Shakespeare, 1778, from which I have mainly quoted (cited as *Prolegomena*).

James Boswell. *Life of Samuel Johnson*, 2 vols. 1791.

Edmond Malone. *Inquiry into the authenticity of certain papers attributed to Shakespeare, Queen Elizabeth, and Henry, Earl of Southampton*, 1796 (cited as *Malone Inquiry*).

W.H. Ireland. *An authentic account of the Shakespearian manuscripts*, 1796.

George Chalmers. *An apology for the believers in the Shakespeare-papers which were exhibited in Norfolk Street*, 1797 (cited as *the apology*).
A supplemental apology for the believers in the Shakespeare-papers . . . being a reply to Mr Malone's answer which was early announced, but never published; with a dedication to George Steevens, and a postscript, 1790 (cited as the *Supplemental Apology*). Facsimile edition by Arthur Freeman, 1971.

John Payne Collier. *Extracts from the registers of the Stationers' Company or works entered for publication between the years 1557 and 1570*, 2 vols. Shakespeare Society 1848 and 1849: Additional extracts in *Notes and Queries* 1861 and 1863 (cited as *Collier, Extracts 1848* etc).

C.R. Rivington. *The records of the Worshipful Company of Stationers*, 1883 (cited as *Rivington Records*).

Edward Arber. *A transcript of the registers of the Company of Stationers of London 1554–1640*. 5 vols. 1875–95 (cited as *Arber*).

Court Books of the Stationers' Company N:P.V.W. (cited as *Court book P* etc).
Entry Book of Copies: A 1554–96 known as and cited as *Register A*): B *1557–1596* (known as and cited as *Liber B) C 1595–1620* (known as and cited as *Liber C*).

The orders, rules and ordinances of the Stationers' Company, 1678 (also known as the *byelaws*). *The charters and grants of the Company of Stationers . . . containing a plain and rational account of the Freemen's rights and privileges . . .* printed by Richard Nutt, 1741 (cited as *Nutt, charters*).

John Lewis. *Life of Mayster Wyllyam Caxton of the Weald of Kent . . .* 1737.

Thomas Langford. *Catalogue . . . of the collection . . . of Joseph Ames*, 5 May and further 7 evenings, 1760 (cited as *Langford*).

Arrowsmith & Bowley, third part of the library of William Herbert. 21 November and four following days 1798 (cited as *Arrowsmith & Bowley*).

Secondary sources

Franklin Dickey. 'The old man at work', *Shakespeare Quarterly* Winter 1960 pp.39–47 (cited as *Dickey*).

S. Schoenbaum. *Shakespeare's Lives*, 1972 (cited as *Schoenbaum*).

References

1. n.d. (1740s) Dibdin I, p.36.
2. John Lewis (1675–1747), author of the first attempt at a scholarly life of Caxton (1737) and of *An essay towards the history of printing in England*, 1739.
3. L.A. V, p.258 and repeated by Dibdin.
4. George Psalmanazar (1679?–1763) known as the 'false Formosan' on account of his spurious *Description of the island of Formosa . . .* 1704.
5. *The general history of printing*, 1732, is of no scholarly value, though it remains a curiosity for its perpetuation of the so-called 'Corsellis myth' that not Caxton, but a mythical Dutchman, Corsellis, was England's first printer.
6. As (3) above.
7. L.A. V, p.257 and repeated by Dibdin.
8. As (7) above.
9. William Blades (1824–90), Caxton scholar and printer, castigated Bagford for being a 'biblioclast' who 'mained old books' in order to make a collection of titlepages. See Blades: *The enemies of books* and letters to Bradshaw in the University Library, Cambridge. Bagford has since been vindicated by T.A. Birrell and Margaret Nickson (see p.37, n.16 below).
10. As (8) above.
11. Ames 159.
12. Ames: preface (unnumbered).
13. Henry Bradshaw (1831–86), Cambridge librarian, to F.A.G. Campbell, Royal Librarian at The Hague, 1 Nov 1874. W. & L. Hellinga. *Henry Bradshaw's correspondence on incunabula 1864–1884*, I, pp.180–81.
14. In Langford's sale catalogue, annotated *Ames*, lot 1298, sold for £3 1s, the copper plates, blocks and copyright, lot 1299, for £5 15s 06d, Maunsell's catalogue, lot 977, for 2s 6d. The marked-up catalogue is now in the British Library.

15. Dibdin I, p.79.
16. Dibdin I, p.78.
17. L.A. III, p.733.
18. Herbert: advertisement to preface. Dibdin I, p.53.
19. Court book N 215.
20. Court book N 221.
21. I am indebted to Anthony Lister for this information and for his reminding me that W.A. Jackson recounts what happened to *annotated Herbert* between its coming into Dibdin's hands and being offered to the Museum in *Records of a bibliographer*, 1967, p.57. He had previously given this account to the Grolier Club, New York, in 1935.
22. Annotated Herbert I, p.877.
23. Annotated Herbert III, p.1342.
24. L.A. VII, p.177.
25. Court book V ff.493–57 29 April 1842.
26. Dickey, pp.39–47.
27. Dibdin I, p.69.
28. Ames pp.306–7.
29. Herbert II, pp.877–82.
30. Ames, p.435.
31. Herbert II, pp.1299–1301.
32. H.R. Plomer. *Dictionary of printers and booksellers ... 1557–1640*, 1910, pp.252–3.
33. Herbert, preface, p.x.
34. Annotated Herbert II, p.814.
35. Dibdin I, p.88 + note.
36. Boswell I, p.389.
37. As above I, p.334.
38. Collier *Extracts ... 1849*, preface.
39. *Prolegomena*, 1788, p.295.
40. Court book P 177.
41. *Prolegomena* p.296.
42. As above.
43. Court books O 116 & 127, and P 399.
44. Court book P 503. This must refer to Alexander Chalmers, not George. 'Mr Nichols stated that several of the principal Booksellers of London and Westminster were preparing an edition of the English Classics and requested that the Court would permit Mr Chalmers the Editor to inspect the Company's Books of Entries of Copies.' Whereas the *Dictionary of National Biography* says of Alexander Chalmers, 'no man ever edited so many works as Chalmers for the booksellers of London', George Chalmers was never involved in anything of the sort.
45. W.H. Ireland, *An authentic account of the Shakesperian manuscripts*, 1796.
46. Preface to the *Supplemental apology*, facsimile edition, 1971.
47. Schoenbaum.
48. Court book P 287.
49. There are two marked copies of this catalogue in the Bodleian, one being Douce CC 393(4). I am indebted to Giles Mandelbrote for looking these up for me when I was unable to get to Oxford to check for myself.
50. Court book V, see n.25 above.
51. C.R. Rivington, *The records of the worshipful company of Stationers*, 1883.
52. Dickey, pp.39–40.

53. Section X 'The Master of the Revels', pp.192–266: XII 'The Chronology of Shakespeare's Dramas', pp.266–494: VIII 'Shakespeare's Note of Hand', pp.144–7.
54. Section VIII, pp.144–7.
55. Notebook A, note tipped in, p.161.
56. *Supplemental apology*, p.469.
57. S. Schoenbaum:
58. Dickey, p.39.
59. *Extracts* ... 1848, preface.
60. Dickey, p.44.
61. *Extracts* ... 1848.
62. Arber *transcript* I, p.xviii.
63. Dickey, p.44.

Discussion following the paper
Contributors – Alison Shell, Anthony Lister, Charles Rivington, Michael Turner, Michael Harris and John Barnard.

Referring to the range of interests of the early scholars using the Stationers' Company records Robin Myers pointed out that they were primarily concerned with Shakespeare and the early printers. In any case access to the Court Books would not have been permitted. Discussion of the tampering with material by John Payne Collier was followed by comments on the printed accounts of the company by John Nichols and C.R. Rivington. In the follow-up Charles Rivington described the strong and continuing links between his family and the company. Robin Myers pointed out that after the publication of Arber access was less restricted. However, even today practical difficulties meant that the records themselves were not easy to get at. The new microfilm edition (published by Chadwyck-Healey) has opened them up to a general readership for the first time. Discussion then moved to the difficulty of reconstructing the past routine organisation of the company even with access to the records. A number of anecdotes were cited which reflected on this, for example, the death of a liveryman at the Hall in the early 19th century, and Benjamin Tooke as Treasurer, keeping the company's money under his bed at the Hall in the 17th. Charles Rivington also drew attention to Charles Knight's account of 'Almanack Day' as a useful source of information. However, it was generally agreed that it was very difficult to work such occasional fragments into a coherent view.

The earlier bibliographers of Quakerism

DAVID J. HALL

'W HO HAVE WROTE more than the Quakers?' was a hostile and rhetorical question asked by one prominent apostate opponent, Francis Bugg.[1] The sheer volume of early Quaker publications justified several attempts to create more or less official bibliographies of British Quakerism between 1708 and the second half of the 19th century. The aim of this paper is to describe those attempts. After the heady days of its mid-17th century origins it was not long before the Society of Friends began to lay emphasis on the maintenance of records and on the accurate chronicling of its history. By the early 18th century it was clearly desirable to have some definitive listing of what had appeared in print. The decision to maintain a reference collection in London, both of books by Quakers and of books written against them, had been taken in 1673 by the Morning Meeting, a weekly meeting of men Friends 'in the ministry' begun in that year.[2]

Three individuals deserve especial, if not quite exclusive, mention in any account of Quakerism's bibliographers – John Whiting, Morris Birkbeck and Joseph Smith. Others contributed to or collaborated in their achievements but there can be no doubt that theirs is the main claim to fame in this specialised area of Quaker history. It seems unlikely that most readers will have heard of anyone in the field other than Whiting and Smith. The work of the three individuals spans almost two centuries. While Friends were certainly well served by their bibliographers it was because of the accuracy and comprehensiveness of their work rather than any great originality of method or contribution to the development of bibliography at large. A little will be said later about contemporary bibliographies of other denominations.

The story proper begins with John Whiting but one earlier unpublished work is relevant in demonstrating the Morning Meeting's concern with its task of ensuring accuracy and consistency in newly printed or reprinted texts as well as with controlling the acceptability of their content. Following the death in 1691 of the outstanding Quaker leader George Fox arrangements were made, in accordance with his instructions, to publish his major works. Three folio volumes appeared between 1694 and 1706.[3] Fox had kept lists of his printed works for himself and some lists of manuscripts existed but before the appearance of the second and third volumes new lists of what was available to the editors were prepared, drawing too on the replies to a questionnaire sent to the counties. These lists, amounting to about 300 pages, survive and, admirably edited by Henry J. Cadbury, have been published as *The Annual Catalogue of George Fox's Papers*.[4] The original catalogue was prepared over a period of about four years by a clerk employed by the Society, Mark Swanner. Many papers were in print either in separate versions or incorporated in Fox's *Journal* but 400 more were printed in the 1698 *Epistles*. With the publication of the three volumes the manuscript catalogue will have been less obviously useful, though it would be interesting to know whether or not Whiting made use of it once he had moved to London.

John Whiting (1656–1722) is the only one of the three principal characters in this account who figures either in a biographical entry of his own in *The Dictionary of National Biography* (Joseph Smith is cited as a source) or in the more general histories of Quakerism.[5] His partly autobiographical work published in 1715, *Persecution Expos'd, in some Memoirs relating to the Sufferings of John Whiting, and many others of the People called Quakers*, is a valuable source for the history of Friends in the period 1679–96. Apart from first-hand observation it was based on the published accounts of which Whiting demonstrated such a good command in his bibliographical work. A 20th-century non-Quaker historian was to choose Whiting as a good example of a lesser leader of the Society in his account of Quakerism from 1660 to 1688.[6] Whiting lived near Bristol until his move to London in 1699. Like many of his contemporaries he suffered considerably for his beliefs but was able to write in prison. In his own catalogue he is shown as the author of eight titles; however Joseph Smith credits him later with 21.[7]

The Yearly Meeting of Friends (the annual assembly of supreme authority, held in London since 1668) asked Whiting in 1707 to prepare a catalogue of Friends' books based on the stocks held by Thomas Raylton, the Society's bookseller and printer, with a view to their acquisition.[8] The intention was also that the catalogue should be printed. The draft catalogue was presented to the Morning Meeting in 1708 and referred by them to a committee for detailed consideration in the first instance.[9] As the work consisted of lists of books it was less liable than most titles to suffer from the Meeting's censorship and it is scarcely surprising that the committee of four Friends reported: 'they have read part of John Whitings Catalogue of friends books and finding it consists of the titles of them, which the said John Whiting was most capable of collecting from the books themselves, which being in his hands, it was therefore thought meet to leave unto his care to fit for the press.'[10] The Morning Meeting decided to recommend to the Meeting for Sufferings (the standing executive body which acted between Yearly Meetings) that 500 copies should be printed.[11] Eight months later the Morning Meeting recorded the receipt of the printed work; 'John Whiting presented to this meeting one of his Catalogues of friends books bound in calf, which this meeting kindly accepts, and it is left with Benjamin Bealing to keep for this meetings use, and Thomas Raylton to take care that the said catalogues ordered as agreed for at the Yearly Meeting to be sent to the counties etc. accordingly.'[12] Two copies were to be sent to each Monthly Meeting of Friends in England and Wales and the remainder of the stock supplied in sheets to Bealing, the Recording Clerk of the Society. In 1709 the Yearly Meeting ordered copies to be sent to four meetings in America and to the Netherlands and Norway.[13]

Whiting's sources for the preparation of his catalogue would have been his own quite significant collection, the collections catalogued in manuscript belonging to the Society and kept at the premises in White Hart Court, Gracechurch Street and the stock held by Raylton which would have included earlier works. Whiting listed over 2600 publications.[14] Recent work on the early literature of Quakerism has produced an estimate of 3759 Quaker publications issued up to 1700 and only 62 in the next decade while a 19th-century estimate based on Smith's *Catalogue* was 6092 up to 1700.[15] Whiting knew of and noted in a supplement upwards of 100 titles needed to complete the Friends' collection. He took as his text *Isaiah* 30.8 – 'Go, write it before them in a table and note it in a book, that it may be for the time to come.' The published work was entitled *A Catalogue of Friends Books: Written by many of the People, called Quakers From the Beginning or First Appearance of the said People. Collected for a General Service, by J.W.*[16] The work ran to 240 pages in octavo including five pages of addenda and three supplements, one of them a list of books in high and low Dutch explained as follows:

Several Volumes, &c. of Dutch-Books coming to my Hands, since the Writing the foregoing Catalogue; by which I perceived many of our Friends Books have been Translated into Dutch (as well as Latin and French) more than I have Noted in the foresaid Catalogue; but these following I cannot find were ever in English, which I thought meet to insert here; in hopes it may stir up some or other to Translate them into English, as there may be a Service, and Opportunity presents.

Since Whiting's preamble to his catalogue presents the best evidence for his methods it will be quoted in full:

The Reader may observe the Method of the following-Collection. First, The Authors 2d or Sirnames are carried on Alphabetically, and the Places of their Birth or Habitation, as far as known. Then the Titles of the Books or 1st Words to the Break-and then Contracted for brevity and further Explanation; and all that are not in 40. (as most are) noted 80.120.fo. for Folio, and B for Broadside, at the End of the Title. Next, the Dates of them, that have any, when Printed and the several Editions as near as I could, and if any have two Dates, the 1st is when Written, and the 2d when Printed, in order of Time under every Author's Name, and not always perhaps as they stand in some of their Works. Then the Number of Sheets; and lastly, the Time and Place of the Author's Death, if known.

Some are set down twice for the more Ready finding them, as some that have two Authors under both their Names, and some not only under the Authors Names, but also under the Title, King and Parliament, Sufferings and Testimonies of, and concerning Friends deceased, because they fall Properly under those Heads; and there they may be found all together what have been written on those Subjects.

And such as have no Authors Names may be found under the Title Nameless, Friends and Quakers, being in the Names or behalf of the said People.

As to the Use or Service hereof, besides the General Notice of what Friends have Written (or Printed) on Truth's Account and their Country, & time of the Death of the Chiefest of them. Hereby may be seen, not only what Books have been Printed of the Sufferings which many of the said People underwent, but also the many Warnings to the Governments and Rulers, &c. Concerned. Which may be Warning to them that Come after. All which is Dedicated to the Service of the Truth, by a Lover of it.

Whiting's *Catalogue* remained the basis of any approach to the study of the literature of Quakerism until the publication of Smith's *Catalogue* 160 years later. Individuals annotated copies and sometimes had them interleaved to allow for additions and these were the essential working tool of those concerned with past Friends' publications. In the 1731 manuscript catalogue of the Society's own collection there is the note: 'And that to make those Collections farther useful recourse may be had to John Whiting's printed catalogue.'[17]

The antiquary William Oldys, himself an editor of the (sale) catalogue of the Harleian library, wrote: 'Honest John Whiting has surely in this work quite borne away the garland, and left it a choice legacy to painful librarians, and as a looking glass even to learned academies.'[18] He expanded on this opinion in a statement about the Friends' Library:

The Quakers have been some years gathering a library, but where reposited I hear not (but the Baptists have one at Barbican). One of their brethren named John Whiting, a man of good intelligence and assiduity, has published a Catalogue of all the Friends' Books, such as Naylor, written by that fraternity; it makes a moderate octavo, and was printed 1708. In my opinion 'tis more accurately and perfectly drawn up than the Bodleian Library at Oxford is by Dr Hyde, for the Quaker does not confound one man with another as the scholar does. Besides, the Quaker is so exact and satisfactory, that he not only gives you the title ample enough, and the size and the town where printed, but the number of sheets or leaves every distinct Treatise contains, from the largest folio to the least pamphlet; and besides all that, what place every author most considerable among them was of, when and where he flourished, and died. Francis Bugg, the notorious revolter from, and scribbler against them, had the best collection of their writings of any of the Brethren; but I think I have read in some of his rhapsodies that he either gave or sold it to the library at Oxford.[19]

Francis Bugg used Whiting's *Catalogue* (his own entries were to take up 15 pages in Smith's though the titles are lengthy) as the basis of an assault on the amount of pernicious Quaker literature, estimating that it contained details of some 4269 publications he wrote:

Multiply this 4269 by 1000, the number of books in each impression, and they amount to 4,269,000 books – a number great enough to poison ten nations, . . . and if they be not timely prevented may, for aught I know, prevail as Mahomet once did over the Greek Churches, &c. I have multiplied their books but by 1000 to an impression, though they often print more, but seldom less; – for instance, R. Barclay's Apology (as I was told) they printed 12,000 of the last impression – 2000 to sell, and 10,000 to give away to Parliament, Lords and Commons, bishops, judges, justices, &c.; for they have a public fund to support them therein, and when that fails, then they rob the poor's box, as I have showed . . . ; so that they have given gratis sometimes fifty on a day while we sit still, and but few oppose them which has sorely grieved me . . .[20]

This is not the place to examine the accuracy of Bugg's assertions in detail but a small sample of the quantity of books or pamphlets ordered to be printed by the Morning Meeting between 1678 and 1698 showed five orders under 1000, three at 1000 and three over 1000 to a maximum of 1500. Apparently 6606 copies of the

1701 impression of Barclay's *Apology* were ordered; 'the last impression' would have been 1703 and the printing figure has not been traced but perhaps Bugg's informant amalgamated the two.[21]

Whiting was a collector as well as a chronicler. In accordance with the terms of his will his widow offered his books to the Morning Meeting and the Meeting for Sufferings in 1724. In 1726 she 'sent in a parcel of her late husband's books' amounting to 29 volumes.[22] This does not quite tally with the substantial collection listed in a manuscript volume now in the Friends' House Library 'A Table of Titles of Tracts in 43 volumes, the Gift of the Widow Whiting'. They were, according to the title-page of the Table, bound up at the charge of the Meeting for Sufferings and the collection comprised more than 1094 tracts and three single volumes.

Morris Birkbeck built on Whiting's work and brought it up to date without publishing his results. Born in 1734 he was to move to America and purchased an estate in North Carolina. He returned to England and by 1784 was involved as a principal in an insurance business in London; the latter part of his life was spent in Guildford in Surrey where he died in 1816. His half-brother William was father of Dr George Birkbeck, one of the founders of the Mechanics' Institution and of University College London. Morris was a regular attender at the Yearly Meeting of Friends in London and had been acknowledged as a minister in the Society of Friends in 1776.[23] A contemporary view of him as a businessman is given in the journals of James Jenkins:

about the year 1778 . . . the firm of Birkbeck, & Blakes became considerable Insurance-brokers, and agents for the sale of goods on commission, first in East-cheap, and afterwards in Great St. Helens Bishopsgate . . . From his partner, [Birkbeck, Blakes] . . . derived but little more aid than that which the use of his name afforded, for, his time and attention were much absorbed in Society-business . . . to pursuits of a commercial nature I do not apprehend he was ever much qualified either by habit or inclination.[24]

At first sight Smith's *Catalogue* contains details of a number of publications by Birkbeck but unusually manuscripts are included and only three items were printed. One of these, *A Tender Expostulation with the less diligent attenders of Meetings for Worship among the Society of Friends. With a few Remarks on the Use of Idolatrous Terms*, was published in London in 1812, in New York in 1816 and in Warwick in 1826.

Isaac Sharp, Recording Clerk of the Society from 1890 to 1917, described Birkbeck as 'a collector and donor of books; a reader and commentator; a maker of catalogues'. The catalogues are of greatest relevance here and while it is not possible to reconstruct either Whiting's or Smith's preparatory work there is evidence for Birkbeck's. Birkbeck naturally began with Whiting's *Catalogue*. His copy, or rather his chief copy, of Whiting is dated 1780, it is interleaved and heavily annotated in both pencil and ink.[25] A note dated 1797 reads: 'I want in this catalogue 279-marked (want) & for the London Library-243-marked (L).' The Library at Friends' House (it had moved from White Hart Court to Devonshire House and thence in 1926 to the Euston Road) has half a dozen notebooks or sheaves of papers of Birkbeck's as well as versions of the finished catalogues in four volumes. Birkbeck had the fortunate habit of initialling many of his notes and dating some of them. The earliest notebook is dated 1791 and is a list of books wanted both by the Friends' Library and Birkbeck himself, based on the system of Whiting's 1708 Catalogue (the Society had issued a printed list of desiderata in 1778). Birkbeck also happened to own Bugg's copy of Whiting. This 1791 notebook contains 28 pages of closely written lists with a number of deletions as items were acquired. There were then 627 titles represented in neither collection except by a handful designated 'bad copy' and 1129 items where Birkbeck's note says: 'I have 1 copy or more of the pieces below but want the following eds. for self or London &c.'

A quarto list of items dated up to 1799 is described as: 'A List of Publications posterior to J. Whiting's Catalogue 1708 Down to the year 1799 and not then to be found in the Library but to be procured if they can be.' A note dated 1800 and initialled by Birkbeck is tipped in. It must refer to the Friends' Library and then to the production of the earlier version of his finished catalogue:

... it remains to separate the duplicates, such as can conveniently be taken away, which will reduce the stock; so many of a sort being an encumberance. 2 of John Whiting's catalogues to be cut, pasted & interleaved so as to afford a blank leaf at least for every page of letter-press with a tolerably large margin. MB has mentioned it to W. Phillips, who waits J.G.B.'s instruction, having a man on the spot, ready to do it properly.[26]

This is the only evidence for outside help used by Birkbeck. The process resulted eventually in what is now a substantial quarto volume of 663 pages including the blanks and at the end, just as in Whiting's *Catalogue*, 20 unnumbered pages listing Dutch books. The binding is not contemporary and a later author index has been bound in. The first original leaf of the text carries the inscription: 'This catalogue included publications from the rise of the Society to the commencement of 1820 by Morris Birkbeck and Thomas Thompson'. We shall return to Thomas Thompson. There are inserted sheets on later paper in different hands.[27]

That volume seems to have been superseded by an entirely manuscript volume of some hundreds of pages with Whiting's entries transcribed. This is almost certainly the catalogue of the Society's Library. There is an explanatory note tipped in about the physical arrangement of the books. Nor does the earlier volume seem to be simply a catalogue of Birkbeck's own collection as it corresponds much more closely to the later one than to the listings of Birkbeck's collection recently published.[28] Both carry annotations in Joseph Smith's hand demonstrating their continued use up to the publication of his *Catalogue*. The later manuscript catalogue is entitled 'A Catalogue of Friends Books written by members of the Society...compiled by John Whiting, Morris Birkbeck, Thomas Thompson. Liverpool, 1836'.

There were two minor catalogues as well and some preparatory work for them survives. Birkbeck was especially interested in works written against the Quakers and produced a catalogue of these as well as of the miscellaneous books not by Friends in the Library including bibles and law books. An undated small quarto notebook of 92 pages is endorsed 'Rough Catalogue (Adverse)' on the cover and titles that Birkbeck had promised to the Library are marked. The main catalogue of adverse books entitled 'Adverse Books or Books written against the Society of Friends' is dated 1806. This time it was Birkbeck's list of his own collection which he presented to the Library but he noted also the titles he had come across but did not own and, like Smith later, he gave details of the answers to adverse books published by Friends. This is supplemented by six leaves in a separate notebook (on 1807 Whatman paper) headed 'Adverse Tracts wanting for the Library at Devonshire House'. The miscellaneous catalogue was preceded by a draft too which included the adverse books. A note written on this implies that it was carefully preserved once superseded: 'The rough drafts, or lists of miscellaneous books including such as are adverse, or otherwise, in Friends Library London; from which the Alphabetical arrangement was finally made, in the Catalogue entitled *Miscellaneous*; now bound and placed there, by M. Birkbeck, 1801.' The catalogue of miscellaneous books 'not inserted in the General catalogue of Friends Books' comprises 200 quarto pages and is dated 1802. There are later manuscript additions, some in Joseph Smith's hand.

Birkbeck's catalogues were firmly based on Whiting, on the subsequent publications in his own extensive collections and on the Library at the Society's headquarters, Devonshire House in Bishopsgate. He had a tendency to annotate his books and to balance Bugg's earlier comments two of his annotations in copies of Bugg's works may be quoted: 'This is the last I have met with the F.B.'s writing – like many other pieces of his, it carries a *Lie* on the face of it; there scarcely can be a dirtier sheet among all the Filth he had produced'; (in his copy of Bugg's *The Pilgrims Progress from Quakerism to Christianity*) 'perhaps a farago of serious ribaldry beyond almost any other publication'.[29] Thus Birkbeck was not only a bibliographer, he read his books and clearly the annotations he provided would be good reading too.

Having given the adverse books in his lifetime Birkbeck bequeathed his remaining collections to the Society for the completion and improvement of the Library in London with the residue, in actual fact the great bulk of the collection, to be given to Friends in York thus establishing a major Quaker library in the north of England. When it came to the dispersal of his library Thomas Thompson of Liverpool (1776–1861) took a major part. Thompson had certainly collaborated with Birkbeck to some extent and was to complete his catalogues. Thompson was a pharmacist and an avid collector – his Quaker books and manuscripts were important but he also possessed a collection of books relating to the early history of chemistry, and coins, minerals and American autographs. He too gave adverse books to the library, estimating the number at between 130 and 150 by 1817, though his main collection of Quaker literature was sold to the Society in 1829.[30] Thompson naturally used an interleaved copy of Whiting as his own catalogue and carried it around with him; this survives at Friends' House. After Birkbeck's death Thompson was actively engaged in the task of sorting and clearing up his books. His correspondence makes it clear that he had supplied gaps in Birkbeck's collection and claimed that Birkbeck had promised him his duplicates.[31] At about the same time Thompson's help was enlisted by the Meeting for Sufferings in making a complete catalogue of the writings of Friends from the year 1800, building inevitably on Birkbeck's work, and resulting in the first of the substantial catalogues, that to 1820, mentioned above.[32]

The best known (as a bibliographer) of the individuals described here is Joseph Smith. He was born in 1819, educated first at the Coopers' Company school and then from 1829 at Ackworth, a Quaker school in Yorkshire. On leaving school in 1834 he was apprenticed for seven years to a London watchmaker William Grimshaw and then went to work for John Morland of Eastcheap, an umbrella maker. Smith married a non-member of the Society in 1846, was disowned but re-admitted to membership in 1850. More importantly in 1846 he opened a book-shop in Bedford Street, Strand, in partnership with Charles Gilpin (1815–74), later M P for Northampton. After a short period the business moved to 2 Oxford Street, Whitechapel. Smith was attached to the Ratcliff Friends meeting for much of his life and was its clerk from 1857 to 1871. The Meeting for Sufferings employed him at piece rates to arrange the material in the Reference Library at Devonshire House between 1856 and 1892 and he attended to this with varying degrees of regularity. He was not a successful businessman and this employment, close to his heart, probably kept him afloat while his erratic attendance seems to have prevented his being appointed Librarian of the Society despite the quality of his work.[33] Whilst no such appointment was made until after Smith's death, it would have been unreasonable to appoint someone else over his head. Roberts wrote thus of Smith in his *Book-Hunter in London*:

Joseph Smith will be better remembered by posterity as the compiler of a 'Catalogue of Friends' Books', and of the 'Bibliotheca Anti-Quakerana', than as book-seller. He was twenty years compiling the former, and is perhaps one of the most striking illustrations of the wisdom of the theory that the bookseller who wishes to be a success should never read! Joseph Smith is of the Society of Friends, and among his schoolfellows were John Bright and W.E. Forster.[34]

Smith must have begun work on the *Catalogue* when he went into bookselling. He says in his preface that it was the result of 20 years' work. He too would have owned a copy of Whiting and he may have made use of the Friends' Library before 1856 when his part-time work there began, making use of the catalogues prepared by Birkbeck and Thompson. He refers in the preface to being granted permission to copy the manuscript catalogues belonging to the Meeting for Sufferings, a very substantial task. In addition he used the Libraries of the British Museum and Sion College. Individuals whose help is acknowledged included Thomas Thompson, Francis Fry of Bristol – a Friend with a then considerable reputation as bibliographer of the English Bible – and John Thompson of Hitchin: 'who has not only supplied me with much valuable information from his extensive collection of Friends' books, but also given me kind assistance during the progress through the press, and without whose help I believe the desired end would not have been accomplished.'[35] Smith mentions that the books which have passed through his hands in the course of business have been a valuable source of information. He also states here and in the later adverse catalogue that he has many of them in stock. His 1846 catalogue of Quaker books for sale listed 420 items on 18 pages; by 1849 he was offering 1452 items on 77 pages.

A Descriptive Catalogue of Friends' Books or books written by members of the Society of Friends, commonly called Quakers, from their first rise to the present time, interspersed with critical remarks and Occasional Biographical Notices, and including all writings by authors before joining and by those after having left the Society, whether adverse or not, as far as known was published by Smith himself in two volumes in 1867. Its comprehensive title echoes many of those of earlier times in his listings in its anxiety to explain every nicety of his content. The work amounts to just over 2000 pages and was priced at £3.00. According to one estimate it contains details of 16,604 works by 2174 authors.[36] 6092 publications are supposed to have appeared before 1700, rather at variance with the estimates quoted earlier, and 6600 since 1800. This latter figure gives some idea of how much work Smith had to undertake on 19th-century material. A calculation based on a modest random sample supports the estimate for the total number of titles.

It can be argued that Smith's claim, in the title and in his preface, that: 'this Catalogue might not inappropriately be entitled, A Biographical Dictionary of Authors of the Society of Friends, with a chronological Register of their publications &c . . .' implies a rather more comprehensive compilation than is really the case. Certainly Smith attempts to include all the traceable writings of Friends on all subjects and this gives interesting indications of their general range of intellectual and sometimes practical interest. The home towns and dates of death of authors are usually given. Occasional entries do give very useful biographical information. Take the example of William Dyne, author of one slender pamphlet:

†DYNE, William, of *London*. This Friend was in his early days in the Marines, having enlisted at the age of 11 years. He became convinced of the Principles of Friends at Rochester, and attended the meeting there in 1839. The same year he felt it his duty to give up the profession of a soldier, and for which he suffered imprisonment in Millbank Penitentiary, 'Esteeming the reproach of Christ greater riches than the treasures of Egypt,' Heb.xi.26. He was an official on the London, Brighton and South Coast Railway for about 17 years, and is now Superintendent of the Friends' Institute.[37]

The use of the number of sheets, adopted by Whiting in his descriptions, was continued by Smith but the need for quick calculation does become annoying and details of pagination would have been more helpful. The work remains invaluable though and it has yet to be replaced. Wing's *Short Title Catalogue* and the *Eighteenth Century Short Title Catalogue* are necessary to augment Smith and do so considerably. He is perhaps weakest, inevitably, on American and then British provincial imprints. It is unfair to expect modern standards of bibliographical description from an author who was listing 16,000 titles in a form concise enough for publication, indeed for publication at his own risk. The subscribers listed at the end of volume two took 278 copies, Henry Stevens of London taking sixteen.

W.C. Westlake, a Friend and a subscriber, wrote warmly of the work in the *Friends Quarterly Examiner*:

. . . we can honestly commend it as edited on the best principles of a book catalogue; and, from the trial examinations we have been able to give, it appears to be carefully and accurately collated. It contains . . . a large amount of information not elsewhere to be obtained, and we can only regret that the necessary cost of so voluminous a work will keep it from the hands of not a few.[38]

Smith himself claimed that the book 'was to be found in all the *great* libraries from the Vatican to Washington, and was mentioned in each volume of the Dictionary of National Biography that had appeared in his lifetime.'[39] *The Publishers' Circular* review would support him; its tone followed this quotation: 'Mr Joseph Smith's Descriptive Catalogue of Friends' books . . . is a phenomenon in bibliography that should not be passed over without special notice . . .'[40] The review in *Notes and Queries* was calmer but still positive: '. . . it is therefore perhaps not much to be wondered at that he should have produced a work apparently so complete and exhaustive as we believe the present will be found . . . the book may fairly be pronounced one alike creditable to the compiler and useful to the bibliographer.'[41] Richard Garnett, Keeper of Printed Books at the British Museum, wrote to Isaac Sharp after Smith's death:

> I am glad to hear that you are writing on the late Mr. Joseph Smith. He deserves high honour for his bibliographical labours, especially the "Descriptive Catalogue of Friends' Books," and the "Bibliotheca Anti-Quakeriana." Both, and especially the latter, where he had no old foundation to build upon, are models of painstaking and accurate research, and invaluable for the light they throw upon highly interesting but outlying departments of literature, which, but for him, would have been very obscure. At present, any investigator of early Quaker literature may consult Mr. Smith's bibliographies with the assurance of in all probability finding what he requires.[42]

Rather later, Percy Muir in his article on 'English Imprints after 1640' wrote of Smith's 'invaluable record' and of 'having in the course of many weary weeks, waded through these extremely extensive volumes' in a context which did not mean that the weariness was due to any shortcoming on Smith's part.[43]

The two-volume *Descriptive Catalogue* did not represent the end of Smith's labours. A supplement was published in 1893 containing both material published subsequent to 1867 and additional items of earlier date that had escaped Smith's notice before. It is not so far as the former category is concerned by any means exhaustive. The supplement is frequently overlooked and its neglect can lead to inaccurate assertions of 'not in Smith' by booksellers. There are for example a dozen or so additional but pre-1867 entries for Joseph John Gurney and 18 for William Penn.[44] Only Part I of *Bibliotheca Quakeristica, a bibliography of Miscellaneous Literature relating to the Friends (Quakers) Chiefly written by Persons not Members of their Society* was published, in 1883. Its 32 pages of text peter out among the anonymous entries, appropriately enough at the title *The Adieu! A Farewell Token of Christian Friendship.*

Smith's *Bibliotheca Anti-Quakeriana or a Catalogue of Books adverse to the Society of Friends* appeared in 1873 at 18 shillings and contained 474 pages of text. It excluded work by those who had been Friends because they appeared in the *Descriptive Catalogue* and was arranged along the same lines. Answers published by Friends to the hostile works are detailed and locations are occasionally given for books that were not at Devonshire House; they include the Guildhall Library, the British Museum and the Bodleian.

So far, the bibliographers of Quakerism have been discussed without any reference to parallel work by others, for example published bibliographies of other denominations. There is indeed no evidence to show what else they may have consulted though the body of work with similar aims is relatively small. We at least know that the most professional of the Quaker bibliographers, Smith, used other libraries. Until the 19th century there was little to act as obvious inspiration other than some of the 17th-century bibliographies of religious orders or the published catalogues of libraries. Dr Williams's Library is a few decades younger than that of the Friends; it was founded under the terms of the will of Daniel Williams in 1716 and its first printed catalogue appeared in 1727. The earlier printed catalogues follow a traditional format, being arranged by sizes of books and then language by language with their own alphabetical sequences. Though they are the catalogues of the major library of nonconformist literature their usefulness as bibliographical tools is limited by their arrangement. James Darling's *Cyclopaedia Bibliographica* (three volumes, 1854–9) provided a more general bibliography of religion a few years before Smith; in part at least it was also a promotional exercise for the Metropolitan Library, a subscription library run by the compiler.

The bibliography of Methodism might be complicated by the 19th-century divisions among the Methodists. G. Osborn's *Outlines of Wesleyan Bibliography*, 1869, contains details of upwards of 2500 titles. It covers in fact only the works of John and Charles Wesley in 60 pages and then those of other preachers in the Wesleyan connection in a further 148. Apart from the Wesleys there are more than 620 authors. Nothing is said of the collections on which the bibliography is based.

Henry Martyn Dexter's *The Congregationalism of the last three hundred years as seen in its literature ...*, New York 1880, has a substantial bibliographical appendix of 326 pages listing 7250 printed titles and giving brief details of major manuscript collections. Although the lists are arranged chronologically and short titles are given (up to four lines of type) the indices make the book most useful. Locations are given, drawn from a list of 54 libraries including Devonshire House, and Smith's *Catalogue* is among the 16 works of reference cited. The listings go up to 1879 giving 49 works for that year. Secondary historical works containing relevant material are listed.

W.T. Whitley's *A Baptist Bibliography* appeared rather later, in two volumes published in 1916 and 1922 respectively. It has advantages over Smith's work with a clearer layout and giving details of pagination. Whitley mentions two other bibliographies as forerunners, those of Smith and Dexter. In an attempt to 'register everything relevant to Baptist History' it is more comprehensive than Smith but makes it clear that this was made necessary by gaps in the earlier material held by the five main Baptist libraries. Locations are given when possible and 35 libraries are drawn on in all.

There have of course been some later bibliographers of Quakerism too and by way of conclusion some passing mention can be made of them. An attempt to supplement Smith is made by a bibliography submitted by Angela Turner for the Fellowship of the Library Association in 1973 covering the period 1893–1967. This is more limited in scope than Smith but its terms of reference are usefully and carefully defined and the arrangement is on a classified basis. On an entirely different basis there is now *William Penn's Published Writings 1660–1726 An Interpretive Bibliography* by Edwin B. Bronner and David Fraser.[45] This is in effect a study guide to Penn's printed works which goes far beyond the bibliographer's expectations. It accompanies a four-volume edition of surviving manuscripts. In a generous format and with useful accompanying essays it takes 430 pages to describe the 135 titles and their reprints to 1726. There is still no published catalogue to the Friends' House Library but one major American collection at Swarthmore College has had its card catalogue reproduced to give details of over 40,000 volumes published up to 1981.[46]

References

1. *The Quaker's Yearly Meeting or Convocation Impeached...* (London, 1695), p.1.
2. Friends' House Library (hereafter FHL), Minutes of the Morning Meeting, vol.1.
3. *A Journal, or Historical Account of the Life, Travels, Sufferings, Christian Experiences, and Labour of Love in the Work of the Ministry, of that Ancient, Eminent and Faithful Servant of Jesus Christ, George Fox...* (London, 1694); *A Collection of many Select and Christian Epistles, Letters and Testimonies...* (London, 1698); *Gospel-Truth Demonstrated, in a Collection of Doctrinal Books...* (London, 1706).
4. (Philadelphia and London, 1939).
5. See William G. Braithwaite, *The Second Period of Quakerism*, second edition (Cambridge, 1961). Braithwaite cites Smith as a source.
6. C.E. Whiting, *Studies in English Puritanism from the Restoration to the Revolution, 1660–1688* (London, 1931), pp.201–5, 224.
7. His life is described in more detail by Isaac Sharp in *Journal of the Friends Historical Society*, 4 (1907), pp.7–16.
8. FHL, Minutes of Yearly Meeting, vol.III, 1707, p.330.
9. FHL, Minutes of the Morning Meeting, vol.3, 1708, pp.277, 281.
10. *ibid*, p.282.
11. *ibid*, p.283.
12. *ibid*, pp.299–300.
13. FHL, Minutes of the Meeting for Sufferings, vol.XIX, 1709, p.284.
14. Birkbeck's interleaved copy of Whiting's *Catalogue*, including some additions has 2862. C.E. Whiting, p.224, estimated over 2600.
15. Hugh Barbour and Arthur O. Roberts, *Early Quaker Writings 1650–1700* (Grand Rapids, Michigan, 1973), pp.567–76; W.C. Westlake 'Friends' Literature – Past and Present', *Friends Quarterly Examiner* (1868), p.119.
16. Imprint: London: Printed and Sold by J. Sowle, in White-Hart-Court in Gracious-street, 1708. This is the same business as Raylton's. Jane Sowle was widow of Andrew and mother of Tace who married Thomas Raylton in 1706.
17. FHL, manuscript.
18. Sharp, 1907, p.15.
19. *Notes and Queries*, second series, 11 (1861), pp.422–3 quoting from a manuscript of

Oldys in the Hunterian collection, Glasgow. P.L. Heyworth, 'Humfrey Wanley and the "Friends" of the Bodleian, 1695–98'. *Bodleian Library Record*, 9 (1976), prints a letter from Wanley to Bugg soliciting the gift of Bugg's works for the Bodleian and mentioning gifts received from Friends.

20. Quoted by Westlake, p.117. from *Bugg's Quakerism a Grand Imposture*, part III, (London, 1716) p.101.
21. FHL, Minutes of Yearly Meeting, vol.II, p.310.
22. FHL, Minutes of the Morning Meeting, vol.IV, pp.253, 295.
23. His life is described in more detail by Isaac Sharp in *Journal of the Friends Historical Society*, 8 (1911), pp.9–15.
24. Most conveniently available in J. William Frost (editor) *The Records & Recollections of James Jenkins* (New York and Toronto, 1984), pp.492, 549.
25. Now in the Birkbeck Library deposited by Yorkshire Friends in the Brotherton Library, University of Leeds.
26. Phillips was the Society's printer, J.G. Bevan a Friend appointed with Birkbeck to try to fill the gaps in the Society's Library.
27. Sharp, 1911, refers to the work being in two volumes but quotes the same inscription.
28. *Birkbeck Library ... An Alphabetical Checklist* (Leeds, 1981), *Birkbeck Library ... Supplement to the Alphabetical Checklist* (Leeds, 1985).
29. J. William Frost, p.549; Sharp, 1911, p.13.
30. Information from the typescript 'Dictionary of Quaker Biography', FHL.
31. FHL, Portfolio 5, item 78, letter from Thompson to John Eliot, a Friend appointed by the Meeting for Sufferings to deal with Birkbeck's legacy; also a letter from Thompson to William Tuke of York, quoted by Russell S. Mortimer, 'The Birkbeck Library, York' *Journal of the Friends Historical Society*, 53 (1973), p.157.
32. FHL, Portfolio 5, item 95.
33. FHL, Dictionary of Quaker Biography; Isaac Sharp, *Journal of the Friends Historical Society*, 11 (1914), pp.1–10. Sharp knew Smith and there is a full and revealing account of Smith's personality.
34. W. Roberts, (London, 1895), p.189.
35. *A Descriptive Catalogue of Friends' Books* ... (London, 1867) I, p.v.
36. Westlake, p.119.
37. *Descriptive Catalogue*, I, p.551.
38. Westlake, p.121.
39. Norman Penney, 'History and Contents of the Reference Library', *The Friend*, 12 December 1902, p.813.
40. 16 January 1868, p.3.
41. Fourth series, 1, 11 January 1868, p.44.
42. Sharp, 1914, p.8.
43. *The Library*, Fourth series, 14 (1934), pp.167–8.
44. *Supplement to a Descriptive Catalogue of Friends Books* ... (London, 1893), the title follows that of the original after the first three words.
45. *Papers of William Penn*, vol.5 (University of Pennsylvania Press, 1986).
46. *Catalog of the Book and Serials Collection ... Friends Historical Library of Swarthmore College (Boston, 1982)*.

Acknowledgements

I am grateful to the Librarian to the Meeting for Sufferings for permission to quote from records of the Religious Society of Friends. Edward H. Milligan and Malcolm J. Thomas kindly read a draft of this paper and offered valuable comments on it. Laurie Gage made helpful suggestions about bibliographical material on other denominations.

72

Discussion following the paper

Contributors – Jean Archibald, Malcolm Thomas, Robin Myers, Michael Harris, Don McKenzie.

Discussion opened with the assessment of the bibliographies of other nonconformist groups including the Congregationalists whose bibliography, published in 1880, provides locations drawing on 44 libraries. Special reference was made to the new bibliography of John Wesley which forms part of the multi-volume edition of his works (Zondervan, Michigan). David Hall pointed out that Whiting's catalogue was used as a guide for Quakers who could purchase items from the society's printer/bookseller. 500 copies of the catalogue were printed and each Monthly Meeting (a group of three to eight congregations) was expected to pay for two. He stated that in 1708 there were between 500 and 700 individual meetings. However, although many are still in being a number of the Quaker libraries have been disposed of – to the advantage, in one modern instance, of the Lancaster University Library. Discussion then moved on to the interest displayed by Quakers in hostile comment. It was clear that in the 17th century the newspapers were being scanned for this material and a collection was being made of the voluminous and virulent output of Francis Bugg. In reply to a question about current research David Hall identified several scholars working in the field including Hugh Barber and Thomas O'Malley. He also referred to the frequent reprinting of standard 17th-century texts which led to discussion of the reliability of the figures for Quaker publications. In response to a question about known numbers of Quakers around 1700 David Hall replied that there were 40–50,000 in Britain, and smaller numbers on the Continent and in North America.

W.C. Hazlitt and his 'Consolidated Bibliography'

RONALD BROWNE

WILLIAM CAREW HAZLITT was born on Friday 22 August 1834 at 76 Charlotte Street, London. In view of his capacity for self-advertisement it is pleasant to learn that 76 Charlotte Street is now occupied by the offices of Messrs Saatchi and Saatchi, but honesty compels the admission that the street has been renumbered at least twice since Hazlitt's time, when 76 was on the west side between Goodge Street and Tottenham Street.

His grandfather, the great William Hazlitt, had been dead for four years. His father, also William, had married Catherine Reynell on 8 June 1833 when he was not quite 22 years old. William Carew was the eldest of their four children and the only one to survive into the 20th century.

The Hazlitts did not remain long in Charlotte Street. They had two successive sets of apartments in Percy Street before moving, in 1838, to a more permanent abode in Alfred Place, Old Brompton. It was not all that permanent. As the family's fortunes fluctuated so they moved around London. They were mobile but not always, alas, upwardly mobile. It was not until 1854 when Hazlitt senior received an appointment in the Bankruptcy Court that he achieved some kind of financial security. Later William Carew was to blame the uncertainty of these years for his mother's early death. She died in 1860.

His own career can be summarised briefly. After spells at a prep school at Brompton and, briefly, at Mr Mecklenberg's school at Margate, he was at Merchant Taylors' from 1842 to 1850. He tried his hand at journalism and civil engineering and, during the Crimean War, was a supernumerary clerk at the War Office. How effective he was as a clerk is difficult to say. Speaking of his time at Merchant Taylors' he wrote

Writing was an art which I never acquired either then or since, although many of the printers of Great Britain, and a very large number of correspondents all over the world, have made the best of a sort of substitute for the English written character in vogue with me. I shall never forget the mingled despair and contempt which his futile endeavours to educate me in this direction inspired in the breast of an eminent calligrapher, commissioned by my father in after years to qualify me for clerical duties. My chief at the War Office declared that, if he had not had absolute ocular evidence to the contrary, he should have thought that I held my pen with my left foot.[1]

Perhaps the kindest thing to be said about his handwriting is that it was a good deal better than his father's.

In 1855 he obtained a Reader's Ticket at the British Museum. 'My next step was to lose it, and during about twenty years I held none nor was ever challenged.'[2]

His first book, *The history of the origin and rise of the Republic of Venice*, was published in 1858. He entered the Inner Temple as a student in 1859 and was called to the Bar in 1861.

The Dictionary of National Biography says that he married in 1863 Henrietta, daughter of John Foulkes, of Ashfield House, Denbighshire. His own account is: 'When I quitted my father's house in Ovington Square, Brompton, in 1862, my wife and I took lodgings in Buckingham Street, Strand, whence I went into unfurnished apartments at the house of Mr Tilbury the actor in Powis Place, Great Ormonde Street, who from his habit of wearing a white neck-tie, used to be known as the Rev. Mr Tilbury. I was here five months, when I took a house in Addison Road, Kensington.'[3] This was their address until 1881 when they moved to Barnes Common, where they lived until 1910 in a house called *Winterslow* after his grandfather's Wiltshire home. They had two children, a son, inevitably called William Foulkes, and a daughter, Gwendoline Henrietta Catherine, always known as Gladys. Hazlitt died at Richmond, in Surrey, on 8 December 1913.

He gave several, not always consistent, accounts of how his interest in bibliography arose. A conflated version may be attempted. He had acquired a number of books for his researches into the history of Venice. Economic necessity forced him to part with these and he did so at a loss. He became aware of the book trade. In 1857 Henry George Bohn began publishing a new edition of Lowndes's *Bibliographer's Manual* and Hazlitt studied it with interest. It was a work of which he afterwards frequently spoke disparagingly and he had, of course, good reason not to love Bohn, but it does seem to have provided the initial impetus and he soon had thoughts of producing something better. He studied the standard authorities, Ames, Corser, Heber, Herbert, Ritson and the rest. He began to frequent the auction rooms and to make the acquaintance of book sellers, collectors and scholars. It was probably at the Daniel sale in 1864 that he began the habit of taking notes or slips of all titles new to him – a practice which he kept up for the greater part of his life. He made contact with scholars and libraries throughout the kingdom, or – as he preferred to call it – queendom. He was stimulated rather than deterred by the publication of John Payne Collier's *Bibliographical and critical account of the rarest books in the English language* which came out in 1865. He announced his own intentions early in 1866 in *Notes and Queries* of 6 January:

IMPORTANT BIBLIOGRAPHICAL ANNOUNCEMENT.
The Editor of "N. & Q." is so kind as to allow me to make public in the most appropriate quarter my design of bringing out immediately, in monthly parts, a work upon which I have been engaged for several years. The title proposed to be given to this book is, "A Handbook to the Early Popular, Poetical, and Dramatic Literature of England and Scotland, from the Invention of Printing to 1660."
Such a project as the present one will necessarily, in its execution, go in a certain measure over ground which has been occupied already by other labourers in a similar field; but the field is one which has been cultivated in such a manner as to afford rich material for new workers.
Our early literature has very numerous admirers both in the Old World and in the New. It is to these that I appeal for encouragement and support, and I do so with confidence.

One branch of early English literature which, in existing works of reference has been very superficially treated, will receive peculiar attention, and a new prominence to which I think it fairly entitled. I refer to our Popular Literature in the strict sense of that term, and to our Folk Lore, which are bound together by very intimate ties. I shall not scruple to give a large space to TOM THUMB and ROBIN GOODFELLOW; for my purposes, these two heroes are worth more than a cartload of tracts political and polemical. I purpose to enter at large into the bibliographical history of all our Romances of chivalry, all our Jest-Books, all our Drolleries, and all our old story-books.

The light and perishable effusions of past centuries will have a higher fascination for me than the gravest discourses of my most erudite and accomplished countrymen – for this once. I shall do more honour to *Jack of Newbury* and *Tom Long the Carrier*, and *Captain Hind, the Great Robber of England*, than to king, duke, or prelate. I, too, shall be drawn away from Bishop Latimer to Robin Hood.

In my pages will be gathered together and embodied (in a few words) all the latest discoveries in bibliography, and an examination of the contents will, it is hoped, justify completely the undertaking.

I purpose to furnish in the case of all rare important volumes the imprint, and a collation, with a note of the public repositories in which they are to be found.

Further, to supply what, I think it will be granted readily, has been hitherto a want – a catalogue, as perfect as possible, of the works of William Elderton, Thomas Deloney, Richard Johnson, Martin Parker, Richard Tarlton, Laurence Price, George Gascoigne, George Whetstone, John Taylor the water poet, and Andrew Borde.

Surprising as it may appear at first sight, such a task has never *down to this time* been efficiently performed; and the Hand-book will also comprise, among others, new and thoroughly-revised articles under the following heads:–

"Shakespeare," "Drayton," "Daniel," "Bartholomew Fair," "Fairy Tales," "Breton," "Rowlands," "Lodge," "Greene," "Jenner (T.)," "Laud," "Adam Bell," "Ballads," "News," "Earthquakes," "Wonders," "Fires," "Gesta Romanorum."

Hundreds of fugitive pieces, broadsides, and ballads will be indexed for the first time, either under general heads, or under the author's name, where his name is known, and important additions will be so made in very numerous instances to the list of a man's writings. I may adduce, for example, SIR FRANCIS WORTLEY, THOMAS DELONEY, and MARTIN PARKER.

Here and there, rather than break abruptly an useful chronological series, I have allowed myself to carry it down a little beyond the Restoration. Such as been the case with the articles upon the *Drolleries, Bartholomew Fair*, and *Ballads*; and, as far as the last was concerned, it seemed to me that such a course was warranted by the familiar fact, that of this particular kind of literature a vast proportion survives only in reimpressions, bearing date long after the period of original publication.

I shall receive with gratitude any particulars of undescribed editions or of unique books coming within the category to which I have limited myself.

55, Addison Road, Kensington,   W. CAREW HAZLITT.

This gives some of the flavour of Hazlitt's prose style and incidentally illustrates one of his characteristics less endearing to other bibliographers. He was always tinkering with the titles of his books. When the first of the eleven monthly parts appeared in March 1867, published by John Russell Smith in tasteful pink wrappers at 2s 6d or in more sober large paper at 5s, the title ran: 'Hand-book to the popular, poetical, and dramatic literature of Great Britain, from the invention of printing to the Restoration'.

On the whole the work was well received and regarded as a notable advance in bibliography. Most readers were prepared to make allowances for the mistakes and inaccurancies inevitable in a compilation of this sort although Hessey, his old headmaster at Merchant Taylors', wrote to warn him to be more careful with his Latin[4] and Hazlitt's somewhat self-congratulatory preface and his denigration of the efforts of previous bibliographers jarred on some readers.

Most notably he fell foul of the redoubtable Bolton Corney, who had been such a formidable critic of Panizzi in the previous decade. Hazlitt was himself no great admirer of Panizzi but that did not make him any happier with Corney's criticisms and the columns of *Notes and Queries* were enlivened for some months with the sort of acrimonious correspondence which is such a joy to the uncommitted onlooker. On the whole Corney had rather the better of the exchanges and it is just possible that Hazlitt felt some special satisfaction when he was able to write:

I was away, when Mr Bolton Corney's books were sold at Sotheby's, and did not see them. But one was returned by the buyer as imperfect; it was Drayton's *Odes and Eglogs* (1605), and was said to want two leaves. I examined it, and found that it was complete, and had two duplicate leaves with variations in the text. I bought it for £1.11s., and sold it to John Pearson on my way home for £8. 8s.[5]

When completed, the *Handbook* ran to just over 700 pages with entries in double columns. Bound sets were sold at one and a half guineas with the large paper at twice that price. The British Museum, perhaps in the interests of economy, bought three of the unbound sets in addition to its large paper copyright set. Hazlitt afterwards claimed that he had listed about 10,000 items of which about half had been described from personal examination and the rest from correspondents' reports or from earlier bibliographies. One criticism was that despite his original announcement he was rather sparing in providing locations for his entries. This had the disadvantage from his own point of view that for the rest of his life he was plagued by correspondents asking him where to find particular items. Although, since he was also beset by enquirers who could not find in the catalogues of the particular institution items he had designated BM or Bodleian he was perhaps in a 'no win' situation. In the last part he found room for a few additional items and corrections. The multiplication of alphabets had begun.

The compilation of the *Handbook* gave Hazlitt something of a reputation as a bibliographer but perhaps the most important personal consequence was that he made the acquaintance of Henry Huth. Huth was a merchant banker and a bibliophile and by Hazlitt's standards, indeed by any standards, enormously rich. Hazlitt said that he had got as far as K when he made Huth's acquaintance and that thereafter he was made free of Huth's magnificent and growing library. Huth also suggested that Hazlitt should let him know of any interesting books he came across – and this became quite a lucrative business. Hazlitt would dearly have loved a salaried appointment as Huth's librarian but Huth felt that this would be too disruptive of his domestic routine. He did however employ Hazlitt on a number of editorial projects and arranged for him to catalogue the English portion of his library. Hazlitt would have been happy to compile the entire catalogue but Huth was doubtful of his linguistic competence in German and Spanish and entrusted the foreign cataloguing to F.S. Ellis, the bookseller. There was some kind of estrangement between Hazlitt and Huth before the latter's death and Ellis was entrusted with the final preparation of the Huth Catalogue but Hazlitt always claimed responsibility for the English entries.

The years with Huth in the background gave him the opportunity to concentrate on the preparation of his *Collections and Notes 1867–1876*, published by Reeves and Turner in 1876.

In his preface he explains that he is now working on a new principle. Everything is to be described from the items themselves. Tacitly he had shifted the frontiers. He no longer stopped at 1660 but pushed on to 1700 and sometimes beyond; he also increased the subject coverage. That he was already thinking of a cumulated edition is shown by a letter from Huth who wrote on 21 March 1876:

I have no objection to your making up two copies of my Catalogue out of the waste to cut up for bibliographical purposes.

I do not think I should care to have your two books incorporated into one volume, for if I do not find what I want in one, I can look for it in the other. Besides I hope that one of these days (though not very soon) we shall have the contents of these two books, and a good deal more, all properly arranged and digested in one bibliographical work, which with the opportunities you have had ought to be a very useful one.[6]

The loss of income from Huth must have been a serious blow but there was always the British Museum and he carried on collecting titles for yet another series. He turned to Quaritch. As he wrote in 1897:

Mr Quaritch... co-operated with me in the enterprise, which constituted throughout my motive for mingling in the commercial circle, and has enabled me to preserve from the risk of destruction a vast body of original matter. Mr Quaritch cannot have realised any appreciable advantage from publishing my *Bibliographical Collections* from 1882 to 1892; and he left me a perfectly free hand with the printer, saying that his share of the business was to pay the bill and sell the books. I waxed tired of the practical side, when I lost £140 by a single volume of the series.[7]

A letter from Quaritch written on 3 November 1879 shows the negotiations at an early stage:

I see that there will be sold at Hodgson's 25 copies of your Literature of England...£1.11.6.

This implies 1) that you printed too many of that book, and it teaches 2) that you should print ... LESS of the volume now in hand.

Only thus can you keep up the reputation of your books.

You did *not* hit the nail on the head by proposing a lower price you should only print 250 & 20 on L.P. and you would get your price more readily.

Now everybody (or many) will say, I shall wait till the new volume is reduced in price. You can only punish these wretches by underprinting the new volume.[8]

Quaritch is referring to Hodgson's remainder sale of 11 November 1879. Such sales were a regular feature of the late 19th-century book trade. In our own time, with galloping inflation and instant remaindering, it seems incredible that the price of a book could be held steady for twelve years and scarcely reprehensible to consider selective remaindering after such a lengthy period. Nor does it seem likely that many purchasers would be encouraged to take the long-term view and decide to wait twelve years in the hope of a bargain.

Quaritch's advice was not heeded. When the *Second Series of Bibliographical Collections and Notes* was published in 1882 with Quaritch's name in the imprint, the edition was indeed limited – but to 525 copies with 25 being on large paper. This was a grave mistake. On 11 August 1885 Quaritch wrote, almost incoherent in his indignation:

I was extremely annoyed yesterday to hear from you that you had sold over my head the remainder of a book which I published for you within 3 years ago.

Before you effected the sale of a book bearing my imprint & in the fate of which I was deeply concerned I expected you to make me a positive offer before parting with it elsewhere.

A book only 3 years old, a respectable publisher does not sell off as a remainder & if he does previous purchasers of copies have a legitimate right to an allowance; or otherwise the publisher would be stamped as a dishonourable trader.

Your having overprinted the Second Series of your "Notes" an ultimate reduction in the price is unavoidable; but for a year or so – the book should be sealed up to a certain extent, so as to give no cause for public complaint.

In my interest as a publisher & not for profit sake I have bought from Messrs. Reeves & Turner their bargain & I hold their delivery note on Ballantyne in Edinburgh.

You see by this fact how bitterly I was annoyed that your book – the "Second Notes" should so soon be thrown upon the market.

Hazlitt has endorsed the envelope: 'I called on Mr Quaritch and reminded him that he had had the refusal and offered me sixpence a copy.'[9]

The Second Series was dedicated to Hazlitt's father and in the prefatory dedication we find an apologia for his bibliographical endeavours and a statement of his new aims: 'The HANDBOOK PROFESSED TO CONFINE itself to certain sections of our early literature; but the BIBLIOGRAPHICAL COLLECTIONS manifested the far more ambitious and formidable design of embracing the whole of it, except such commodities as mere sermons and the technicalities of controversial theology.' It was in this preface that he calculated that he had so far described 21,000 items direct from the original.

1882 is also the date of one example chosen from many to illustrate Hazlitt's commercial relations with the British Museum. In *Confessions of a Collector* he writes: 'In 1882 there appeared in a catalogue published by the firm [Sotheby's] *The Famous and Remarkable History of Sir Richard Whittington*, octavo, 1650, a mediocre copy, but twenty years earlier than any on record. I left a commission of five guineas and the lot fell to me at as many shillings'.[10] What he does not add is that he sold it to the Museum a few weeks later for 5 guineas. He later claimed with some justice that he was one of the four individuals who had done most to fill the gaps in the Museum's early English collections. The other three were Maskell, Halliwell and Henry Stevens.

Soon however there was to be a different aspect to his relations with the Museum. In 1883 Eugene Roy, an Assistant Keeper, or in more modern terms, a Deputy Keeper, died and Hazlitt saw himself as the ideal successor; besides, a reliable income would be very useful. He wrote to all his influential friends and, frequently, to Edward Bond, the Principal Librarian. He received support from Lord Derby and Lord Spenser. But there were 26 candidates including Edmund Gosse, who was tired of working at the Board of Trade. Richard Garnett wrote to Gosse that while he personally would welcome the possibility of having him as a colleague again, the appointment of an outsider would be so unpopular with the existing staff that Gosse could not hope to be happy there.[11] How much more would this have applied to Hazlitt with his strong views on the Museum's cataloguing policy.

On 4 December Bond wrote to Hazlitt to inform him that Russell Martineau, the distinguished orientalist, had been promoted to fill the post.[12]

This was not quite the end of Hazlitt's aspirations. Four years later Bond himself was due to retire. Stubbs, the great medieval historian, whom Hazlitt had known as Librarian at Lambeth Palace, and who had in 1884 exchanged a Regius chair at Oxford for an episcopal throne at Chester, told Hazlitt that he had been in touch with the Archbishop of Canterbury pointing out Hazlitt's merits and qualifications. Nothing came of this episcopal initiative nor had Hazlitt any success in 1885 when he tried to become Secretary of the Society of Antiquaries. Henry Stevens wrote to him: 'As your handwriting appears to be that of an Antiquarian, and can be read as well as studied by experts, I think you may be safe in going in for the post. There will probably be about a thousand other Applicants, as a good house, salary and position accompany the office.'[14] If he couldn't find a job he could at least press on with his bibliographical collections. Relations with Quaritch were patched up and in *Book-Lore* for October 1886 appeared a letter from T.N. Brushfield which was to have unexpected consequences.

THE announcement recently made, that Mr. Quaritch was about to publish another volume of bibliographical lore, prepared by Mr. W. Hazlitt, is one of much interest to the book-loving world. As this will be the fourth consecutive volume on the subject by the same indefatigable author (the previous ones having respectively appeared in 1867, 1876, and 1882), a great boon would be conferred on bibliographers and literary men generally if there could be added, as an appendix to the forthcoming work, a general index (no matter how brief) of the names and subjects contained in the four volumes. Under present circumstances, as there are two separate alphabetical lists in each – and the one to appear shortly will not, probably, in this respect differ from its predecessors – no less than eight separate references will have to be made before it can be ascertained whether the special work sought for is noted in them or not. Much time, inconvenience, and, I think I may add, temper would be saved by the publisher carrying out a plan of this kind, and so earning the thanks of the literary world, for which he has so long catered.

T.N. BRUSHFIELD, M.D.

Salterton, Devon, 13th September, 1886.

Within a few days Quaritch received a letter from George Gray, of Cambridge, which he passed on to Hazlitt:

In *Booklore* there is a very good suggestion with reference to the forthcoming work of Mr. Hazlitt's with which I fully agree. If you have not arranged for such an index to the 3 books and it is your wish or Mr. Hazlitt's that there should be an index, I shall be glad to make it for you, the only reward I should require would be a reference to me in the Preface, and a copy of the work.[15]

Quaritch, who knew a bargain when he saw one, suggested that the offer be accepted on condition that it included the forthcoming volume as well.

There followed what must have been a trying time for Gray. The 'Third and Final' series duly appeared in 1887 in an edition limited to 270 copies, 20 being on large paper, and an announcement of Gray's index in the preface. Two years later came 'Supplements' to the third and final series with a prefatory note that the index had been delayed by Gray's indisposition and an assurance that these items would also be included in the index. In the preface Hazlitt disclaimed any intention of dealing thoroughly with Quaker literature because the Society had its own excellent bibliographer.

Later in the same year supplementary material appeared in three consecutive issues of the *Antiquary*. These too were indexed by the indefatigable Gray. Hazlitt, of course, had the last word. A second 'Supplement' appeared in 1892.

When the Index finally appeared in 1893 Hazlitt tacked on an appendix of additional entries. He also stated categorically in the preface: 'Here my system of periodical issues of the result of my studies of the bibliographical product of the auction rooms and of the stores of my good friends the booksellers must terminate.' He was not to shake off his addiction so easily.

1893 was a bad year for Hazlitt. In November he sold a number of his grandfather's books and manuscripts and many more of his own books in a two day sale which realised £1810. 18s. 6d.[16] On 20 December we find that delightful New England writer, now largely forgotten, Louise Imogen Guiney, writing to Richard Watson Gilder, the Editor of the *Century* magazine:

May I ask whether you happen to know of any New York daily or weekly which is in need of a first-class London correspondent? Mr. William Carew Hazlitt is anxious to find such a one, which will make permanent arrangements. I wonder if you know him? He is grandson of Hazlitt the Great, though that is neither here nor there, except as *my* reason for liking him; He is a thorough-paced literary man of fifty-six or so, editor and author of innumerable books, and in constant touch with general affairs outside literature...I would give a good deal to be able to see him rightly placed, especially just now.[17]

Miss Guiney had made Hazlitt's acquaintance because of her devotion to 'Hazlitt the Great'. There are several of her characteristic letters in the Hazlitt correspondence in the British Library although only one has been included in the two volumes of her published letters. On 29 May 1897 she was writing in rather less charitable tone to Herbert E. Clarke:

C.H. [Carew Hazlitt] lately wrote a too tender-hearted friend of mine, T. Whittemore of Tufts College, a rather distressful appeal to buy up dozens of his committed (and unrepented) Prose Works. It sounded as if Grandson might be at his wits' end for tomorrow's dinner; for which I am sorry enough. But if the world is hard on him, it is only because he has always turned so sour a face towards it.[18]

Whatever Hazlitt's financial difficulties between 1893 and 1897, he was still amassing bibliographical material and he was still hoping for a cumulated edition. In 1898 he approached the Royal Historical Society without success[19] and he consulted A.W. Pollard, Secretary of the Bibliographical Society.

Early in 1899 Pollard wrote:

The Council of the Bibliographical Society met this week for the first time since you mentioned to me your idea that the Society might print your Bibliographical Collections in a final form, & I thought it right to communicate your proposal to them at once, although I shd have liked to have been able to avail myself of your invitation to see your collections for myself. I had rather hoped that the final consideration of the matter might have been postponed to a later meeting, but the Council felt very strongly that the proposed work would strain our finances too severely for it to be entertained; & this being so they thought it unfair to keep you waiting for an answer. I was therefore instructed to inform you that while cordially in sympathy with your plan, the Council was unable for financial reasons, to undertake the publication, even by instalments, of so large a work. I am afraid that the policy of 'small undertakings' to which they are now adhering, was started by myself, but I am sincerely sorry not to have been able to bring the matter to a conclusion more in accordance with your wishes.[20]

Pollard reopened the matter on 21 March 1905:

I have some reason for thinking that if I were to bring up your scheme again the Council of the Bibliographical Society would be inclined to take a different view of it. I will not, of course, ask you to make us another formal offer of it, but I should be glad to know from you (i) whether you would object to divide the work into two parts, the first including the period up to 1640, the second all your later books, (ii) whether if the services of competent subeditors were obtained who would compare your titles with books at the Museum, Oxford & Cambridge, you would object to this being done. (iii) whether if the Bibliographical Society pledged itself to spend *at least* £200 a year in bringing out the '1640' part in annual instalments till the whole was issued, & then after a little interval to take up the later portion, you would in consideration of this pledge or contract supply it with your slips arranged for publication in a single alphabet, and transfer to the Society the copyright in the whole work, insofar as copyright exists in it.

The division of the Collections into up to & after 1640 I consider essential, as *up to 1640* we want notes of everything: after 1640 only of a selection. The proposal to check your slips involves no slur of any kind on your accuracy, but is a mere carrying out of the Museum standard of two pair of eyes to every title. As to the 200 a year, I name that sum only so as to be on the safe side, but I never yet started a subscription without getting the money I asked for & I think that I could get individual members of the Society to start the thing in a way which would allow of much more rapid progress.

Of course we can neither of us commit ourselves finally till plans are matured, but if you write to me that you see no objection to my three points I will begin to prepare the ground & feel fairly confident that if you will give me a little time I can bring it off.

Then he adds a postscript:

Perhaps this is oversanguine, but at least I could have a try.[21]

It seems probable that Hazlitt was not happy with these conditions. Instead he offered his *Roll of honour*, a list of over 17,000 British book collectors. The Bibliographical Society rejected this, probably regarding it as overrich in characters and sadly deficient in plot. It was published by Quaritch in the following year.

Two years earlier, in 1903, Hazlitt had published a fourth series of his 'Biblio-graphical Collections'. This time Quaritch had his way and the edition was limited to 150 copies. It is a substantial volume although some standard reference works seem unaware of its existence.

The next step was to assemble all the items so far printed, including the English entries in the Huth catalogue, into one alphabetical sequence. They were pasted into nine large guard volumes. The manuscript slips collected between 1903 and 1906 were arranged in a further four guard volumes along with printed entries from Lemon's catalogue of the Society of Antiquaries broadsides and F.G. Ste-phen's catalogue of the engraved broadsides in the British Museum Department of Prints and Drawings.

This scissors-and-paste work seems to have been substantially completed by September 1908 and the resulting 13 volumes constitute the 'Consolidated Bibli-ography'. They were deposited in the Museum probably in 1910 when the house at Barnes was given up. Hazlitt, however, was still making corrections and addi-tions to the manuscript volumes up to a few weeks before his death.

He had already sold most of his books; now he sold his magnificent coin collection and his collection of art and furniture. On 5 March 1912 he made his will. After all, he was 77. It is a lengthy and curious document and much of it relates to his 'Consolidated Bibliography'. He left the reversion of his estate, after the demise of his daughter, to the Trustees of the British Museum. A sum not exceeding £2000 was to be devoted to the completion of various literary projects and in particular the publication of the Bibliography. The residue was to be invested and the interest applied to augment the funds available for the purchase of English books printed before 1640. He urged immediate publication of the Bibliography with 200 copies to be distributed gratis to libraries throughout the world, not forgetting one to the Municipal Library in Maidstone. He also left the Museum annotated copies of some of his other books, his select correspondence and his diary.

On 20 January 1913 he added a codicil. He indicated that he had not given up hope of arranging publication himself, but failing that, the arrangements for the Museum were to stand except that the stipulation about free distribution was abandoned, only 250 copies were to be printed and, pending publication, the work was to be retained in the private room of the Keeper of Printed Books and not made available for public consultation. He died on 8 September. Probate was granted on 4 October and the bequest was reported to the Trustees on 4 December.

The bequest was accepted, with the unfortunate exception of the diary, and G.F. Barwick was asked to report on the suitability of the Bibliography for publication. This he did on 30 June 1914. He suggested publication as soon as possible and the appointment of an outside editor to oversee the work at a fee not exceeding £500. His proposal was accepted by The Trustees on 14 July but time had already run out and it was inevitable that the Treasury would refuse to sanction the expenditure because of wartime circumstances.

There was some talk of reviving the project after the War, but the Museum had many other preoccupations and nothing came of it. When Miss Hazlitt died on 16 February 1947 publication was no longer a realistic proposition, the Trustees felt that Hazlitt's work was completely superseded and it was found possible to interpret the will in such a way that the whole remaining sum (£7,230. 13s. 7d.) could be invested to form a fund for the purchase of early books. While the Museum Trustees decision in 1948 not to proceed with publication was inevitable, Hazlitt's work was not perhaps as completely superseded as they thought. Even 40 years later it still retains some value. The recent publication of a new edition of 'Pollard and Redgrave' means that the period up to 1640 has been almost definitively covered but it seems that the editors did not fully exploit the 'Consolidated Bibliography'. For the 'Wing' period he is extremely useful. He had, after all, described nearly a third of the extant corpus of English pre-1700 printed material direct from the original items. On the whole his transcriptions of titles are as full and accurate as we have any right to expect. He has recorded a number of items which can no longer be traced. Above all he frequently provides the essential link between 'Wing' and the British Library's *General Catalogue* which will be needed at least until the day the latter is fully machine-readable and properly revised or the former is given something like the ESTC treatment.

Very recently the British Library has microfilmed the 'Consolidated Bibliography'. The five reels of film are more convenient for scholars than the 13 cumbersome guard volumes. Should there be evidence of demand it is possible that copies may be sold to other libraries and after three-quarters of a century Hazlitt may achieve something of the distribution, if not quite the publication, for which he so fervently hoped.

References

1. W.C. Hazlitt: *The Hazlitts*. vol.2. London, 1912, pp.41,2.
2. *Ibid*, p.253.
3. *Ibid*, p.134.
4. BL. Add.MS.38,899. f.334.
5. *Confessions of a Collector*. London, 1897. p.154.
6. BL. Add.MS.38,902. f.164.
7. *Confessions of a Collector*. pp.171,2.
8. BL. Add.MS.38,903. f.58.
9. BL. Add.MS.38,905. f.61.
10. *Confessions of a Collector*. p.165.
11. Ann Thwaite: *Edmund Gosse*. London, 1984. p.536.
12. BL. Add.MS.38,904. f.112. I am indebted to Mr. P.R. Harris for information about Hazlitt's candidature.
13. BL. Add.MS.38,906. f.46.

14. BL. Add.MS.38,905. f.29.
15. BL. Add.MS.38,905. f.107.
16. The catalogue was reprinted by A.N.L. Munby in his *Sale Catalogues of Libraries of Eminent Persons*. Vol.1. London, 1971.
17. *Letters of Louise Imogen Guiney*. Vol.1. New York, 1926. p.52.
18. *Ibid*. p.184.
19. BL. Add.MS.38,908. f.15.
20. BL. Add.MS.38,908. f.33.
21. BL. Add.MS.38,911. f.26.
22. BL. Add.MS.38,911. f.48.

Discussion following the paper

Contributors – Jean Archibald, Katherine Swift, Philip Harris, Robin Myers, Anthony Lister, Michael Winship.

In response to the opening question Ronald Browne said that Hazlitt's diary had probably been destroyed under the terms of his daughter's will. Some surprise was expressed that Quaritch had objected to the remaindering of Hazlitt's book when he was engaged in a variety of similar practices on both sides of the Atlantic. It was suggested that it was conventional practice in the 1880s to retail books at half price two or three years after publication. Ronald Browne added that Quaritch himself was offering Hazlitt's *Second Series* at £1.16s five years after publication. In response to a further question he emphasised the range of Hazlitt's interests which led him to construct substantial coin and art collections, sold off under financial pressure in 1909. His bookselling activities alone produced quite a good return and the evidence for this could be found among the receipts at the British Library. In conclusion discussion centred on the long-term importance of the Hazlitt catalogues. Ronald Browne stressed the value of his full transcripts of titles. His entries offer a valuable link between Wing and the British Library's *General Catalogue*. Although his transcripts contain errors, particularly in the original *Handbook*, many of these were said to have arisen from the supply of faulty information by others and many are corrected in the *Consolidated Bibliography*.

The Bibliographical Society as a band of Pioneers

JULIAN ROBERTS

THE THEME of this conference is 'Pioneers in Bibliography', and I take the liberty of speaking not of a single pioneer, but of a group of them, namely the Bibliographical Society. I believe it is permissible to do so, because to anyone reviewing the Society's history it is clear that the subject of bibliography was, after a slightly shaky start, defined by a group of men who were very close to one another and that their legacy, though now divided with other groups, is still in the Society's hands. How the Society retained this legacy is, perhaps, something upon which I have some qualification to speak, since I was its Honorary Secretary or Joint Honorary Secretary for more than 20 years, and in 1986, prematurely because of the illness and death of Julian Brown, became its President.

A number of sources present themselves to anyone enquiring what the Society is, or was, for. It must be admitted at the outset, however, that a comprehensive series of archives is not among them. Apart from a set of rather uninformative Council minute books, which are – like the rest of the files from about 1961 onwards – with the Society's Library at Stationers' Hall, the only survivor from an earlier period is a single file on the Society's Gold Medal, from which I shall quote later on. Neither I nor my successor have been able to find any others. There is, however, a rich source in the correspondence of the late Graham Pollard now preserved in the Bodleian Library, and I am grateful to Esther Potter for directing me to the relevant part of this.

There is, however, an abundance of printed sources. In the first place there are the statements of the founding fathers of the Society, notably its first President, W.A. Copinger, and the speakers at the Society's earliest meetings. I shall give reasons for believing that the Society changed its direction and composition rather quickly and in an interesting way; the most useful statement of this was in an address given in 1913 on the Society's 21st anniversary by its Honorary Secretary.[1] A.W. Pollard's was a cheerful summary, but he alluded to the measure of international interest, particularly in Germany, that the Society's work had aroused. After that address there is for some time little on its role – perhaps because with the establishment of work on the *Short-Title Catalogue of English Books 1501–1640* (for so it was first called) presaged at the Annual Meeting in January 1917 – 'now that the Society has entered on a new quarter of a century of its life we must form new plans' – and given much clearer shape a year later, the Society had emphatically found itself a role and embraced it eagerly.

It did, however, three years into another war, take stock again upon its jubilee in 1942, though the results of this stock-taking were not published (as *Studies in Retrospect*) until 1945. I shall draw heavily upon *Studies*, not least because of the abiding value of the contributions. *Studies* was edited by F.C. (later Sir Frank) Francis, and it is fitting to remember how much he did to hold the Society together as its Secretary and as Editor of *The Library* during the war. The British Museum and its successor Library also have cause to be grateful to him for keeping bibliography so firmly in the 'curriculum' at the Museum.

The Society's centenary is now four years away. The Council has invited Dr Peter Davison to produce a commemorative volume, and since we all learned the value of Peter Davison's scholarship, combined with energy and efficiency, during his editorship of *The Library* I don't doubt that such a volume will be in your hands on 15 July 1992.

There has been, as you may have noticed, a resounding silence since 1945. When I retired as Joint Honorary Secretary in 1981, it occurred to me then that perhaps I should give some account of my stewardship during a period when the map of bibliography changed completely. However, with the end of one era, marked by the publication of the completed *STC* in 1986, and the beginning of another with the formation of plans for a history of the book in Britain, it seems a good time to begin that account. So there is a certain amount of personal recollection in what follows.

Our founder-President was W.A. Copinger, perhaps now best remembered as the middle term in that incunabular triad, Hain-Copinger-Reichling. He was a lawyer by profession, and a noted book-collector. He had broached the idea of such a society to a Library Association meeting in Reading in 1891, something which underlines the fact that the largest components in the Society's membership have been librarians, together with university teachers of English and antiquarian booksellers. Copinger's inaugural address[2] divided bibliography into areas which would not be recognised today, perhaps because of the rapid expansion of knowledge, whereas Copinger's outlook was essentially historical. But what he was really interested in was a general catalogue of English literature, and in the earliest printed books. Certainly the Society lost interest fairly quickly in subject bibliography and in the bibliography of books *about* particular places; even in the enumerative bibliography of individual authors. Although there are articles about the bibliography of certain subjects in early numbers of the *Transactions* these were always treated historically. The Society has in general avoided publishing author bibliographies; though the egregious Wise and Buxton Forman were to provide exceptions to this as to other rules. This gap in its concerns was very neatly filled, at least since the Second World War, by the *Book Collector*, with its more bibliophilic interests and its links with the 'Soho bibliographies' and their imitators. Copinger was followed in his inaugural address by H.B. Wheatley on *The present condition of English Bibliography and suggestions for its future*.[3] What Wheatley wanted was a massive Bibliography of English Literature, a need that was of course filled by the *Cambridge History* and later by Bateson's great *Cambridge Bibliography* and its successor the *New CBEL*. This is an enumerative and qualitative work, that is, a list of works by people who are judged to be

good together with a list of critical works upon them. But I cannot help remark-
ing that Wheatley's concern about American and Colonial editions prefigures our
own discussions in 1976 about the Eighteenth Century Short-Title Catalogue.
Which leads to a digression.

It was remarked in *Studies in Retrospect*[4] that the early membership of the Society
conspicuously lacked members of the British Museum staff, other than Richard
Garnett, and it was suggested that they found the Society's programme rather
woolly and lacking in direction. But with the recruiting of A.W. Pollard as
Honorary Secretary in 1893, there was forged a link with the British Museum
which was only broken for the four years when R.B. McKerrow was sole Secretary from 1934–38. The British Museum (or British Library) raised the present
President and his predecessor and supplies all the present Officers of the Society
except the Librarian. It has also supplied a large part of its audiences, as there
appears to have been a custom of long standing by which Museum/Library staff
attended meetings without the necessity of being members, having to account
neither to the Museum for the time they were away, nor to the Society for the teas
they ate. It was only to be expected that the work of the Museum and the Society
became intertwined and that the exceptional men recruited to the Museum in the
last 20 years of the 19th and first 20 of the 20th century – I need only cite Pollard
himself, Robert Proctor, Victor Scholderer, Henry Thomas and A.F. Johnson –
should all have been prominent in the Society and have contributed extensively to
the *Transactions*. And I suspect that the urge to date and attribute to printers the
undated and often fragmentary literature before 1556 – a constant problem at the
Museum as I myself found – was a powerful stimulus to much of the Society's
publishing. The source material, the incomparable collections built up under
Panizzi and his successors, ensured that the work of the bibliographically-minded
members of the staff – and the Society – would lie not only with British books, but
with foreign books of all periods, and particularly with the most representative
collection of incunabula in the world. I am sure that the study of books as material
objects was strongly influenced by the way in which other objects were studied
and recorded in the National Museum.

It is clear that the slight air of dilettantism and lack of direction which hung
about the Society in its first year or so was rapidly dispelled under the influence of
Pollard, his colleagues and the young Walter Greg who joined in 1898 and
became a Council member three years later. Greg was, with his Cambridge friend
R.B. McKerrow, the leading theorist of bibliography, as the terse and single-
minded attitude displayed in his presidential address of 1932 and in *Studies in
Retrospect* testify. It is fascinating to see him in the latter anticipating D.F. McKenzie's Panizzi lectures[5] in contemplating the extension of bibliography to the
'phonographic record'.

Nowadays we take the rules of bibliographical description almost for granted,
but in the Society's early days there were no manuals to turn to (such as McKerrow's of 1927 or Bowers' of 1949 or Gaskell's of 1972) and the Society appointed
a small committee of Pollard, Greg and Francis Jenkinson; their thoughts were
published in 1908[6] and were followed by Falconer Madan's article on degressive

bibliography.[7] What is surprising now is the relative lack of interest in collation formulae to which McKerrow and later Bowers rightly attached so much importance.

Five years later Pollard was able to sum up the Society's work in its first 21 years, and he did so in a fairly personal and light-hearted way, as is the wont of Honorary Secretaries on festival days.[8] After reviewing the Society's officers, speakers and contributors, he went on to draw a distinction between the early illustrated monographs, nine of them elegantly printed but all dealing with a foreign subject, and the work which had up to then been done, as he put it, 'to help set in order our own English bibliographical house'. From the beginning of the new century he could report great progress, for Duff's *Century* and two of the Printers' Dictionaries, to 1667, had appeared; the *Handlists of Printers* to 1556 were also to be soon completed.

Pollard had begun his anniversary paper with a tribute to the Society's first President, Copinger, but the best he could find to say about the latter's Supplement to Hain's *Repertorium* was that it was better than nothing, since we were [this in 1913] to get a 'new and satisfactory edition of Hain. With the aid of the Prussian Minister of Education we are to get that edition six or seven years hence'. Pollard is here referring to the *Gesamtkatalog der Wiegendrucke* which, 75 years later, has reached volume 9 and the letter G. The Bibliographical Society has not I think been in the van of incunable studies, though one of its monographs, Allan Stevenson's *The Problem of the Missale Speciale*, long in gestation and a source of some grief to the Secretary, is an epoch-making work both as a study of incunabula and of paper-making; it has however, listened to, and published, many papers, perhaps being content that its members should, in their working hours, compile the *British Museum Catalogue* and its Oxford and Cambridge complements. But the work then in hand in Germany spurred the Society to publish its own bibliography of English incunabula, Gordon Duff's *Fifteenth Century English Books*. It was completed by Henry Thomas from Gordon Duff's notebooks. Gordon Duff, by the way, perhaps the most eminent bibliographer of his day – he was born in 1863 and died in 1924 – had never been more than an Honorary Member of the Society, though as Falconer Madan observed in the obituary in *The Library*,[9] he was the originator of the Society's *Handlists* and during his seven-year librarianship at the John Rylands Library gave that library its true place in bibliographical scholarship, and was a frequent contributor to the Society's *Transactions*. 'His habits were not conducive to long life' wrote Falconer Madan in the obituary.

Pollard's piece also makes it clear that the Society had no firm plans for any English bibliographical work beyond about 1640, and he seems always to have regarded later bibliography as outside the Society's scope. He certainly did so in 1935. He thought however 'with the help of Mr Wise, Mr Aitken, Mr Edmund Gosse and Colonel Prideaux we can hope to grapple successfully with the problems of the eighteenth and nineteenth centuries'. What manner of help was to come from Mr Wise lay well in the future; when the storm burst in 1934 Pollard was to write to McKerrow of his affection for Wise, qualifying this with his belief that Wise had been culpable in handling the forged pamphlets.[10] It must be said also that Gosse's reputation for accuracy did not augur well for bibliography, either.

But this is to anticipate. The idea of a brief record of the output of English presses from 1501 to 1640 seems to have been crystallising in Pollard's mind during the war and was first mooted at the Annual Meeting in January 1918, where Pollard's address[11] described work which had already taken place at the British Museum. At this stage the intention was obviously to produce an arrangement of books under printers or publishers, into which could be sorted entries from the Bodleian and Cambridge. The end-product would be a series of monographs resembling the existing *Handlists*, which only extended to 1556. Since this idea was developed in the next year into what we now know as *STC* and is the Society's single most important contribution to bibliography, I shall follow this thread through to the present day, not just to the revised *STC*, but to other members of its family.

By the following year, 1919, the title, now incorporating the formula 'Short-Title' had been decided upon, an alphabetical sequence rather than a sequence by printers had been settled, a body of helpers enlisted and finance ensured by the generosity of G.R. Redgrave. The specimen printed in the *Transactions*[12] differs little in style from that printed in 1926 and retained for the second edition, though the layout was certainly improved later. The tone of Pollard's paper, summarised in the *Transactions*, is clear and confident, and we who have been involved in later work along these lines can only salute the original compilers. They knew fairly accurately how many books were involved (the prediction in 1918 was about 25,000 editions; since at that stage they had not counted in the 400-odd incunable editions, the total in the end was less than 1000 out, and even that was swelled by a few editions which only existed in the imagination of Mr Jaggard). So it was not surprising that with their accurate estimates, and the work that had already been done at the British Museum, within eight years *STC* was printed and published.

Almost as an afterthought, there are in the *Transactions* three lines appealing for American help, and another four lines recording the offer of help from G.P. Winship and G.W. Cole 'in regard to the numerous early books now in the United States'. For in 1918 no one could have foreseen that the transfer of early English books across the Atlantic would by 1926 have become a flood, utterly transforming the map of scholarship in English bibliography.

Of the many purchasers of *STC* in 1926 one of the youngest must have been William Alexander Jackson, a student at Williams College, already engaged upon a catalogue of the Chapin Library there. When Jackson himself contributed a brief chapter on 'The Study of Bibliography in America' to *Studies in Retrospect* he thought 'unless the flow of importations should be staunched, which does not now seem very likely, it is probable that for some time to come a large part of our bibliographical efforts will be spent in listing and describing the "holdings" of American libraries'.

Jackson did quite a lot himself to ensure that the flood of importations was as little staunched as possible. My own early years at the British Museum were dedicated to the reverse process, that is, to staunching rather than unstaunching, but my colleagues and I were united in assisting him with the revision of *STC* which he had begun before the war and which the Bibliographical Society had formally entrusted to him and F.S. Ferguson in 1949. The history of this revision is set out in the introduction to volume I of the revision, published in 1986, but of course the whole story isn't there. When I became Secretary of the Society, Jackson and Ferguson had got very much out of step, as was to be expected of such very different personalities; Ferguson was indeed preoccupied with the kind of bibliography he had laid down in *Studies in Retrospect* (a matter to which I shall return) and Jackson in fact got little help from him at that time. The final editor, Katharine Pantzer, who took over on Jackson's death in 1964 (Ferguson died in 1967) imposed her own kind of rigorous control on the work. She would prob-ably not disagree with me when I say that one of her own principal interests, the precise attribution of books to printers, was in the end very close to Ferguson's (or rather to part of Ferguson's interests, as we shall see) and indeed to the original concept of the catalogue. She is now working on the Printers' Index, which will not only supplant Paul Morrison's Index, but will go a long way towards sup-planting Duff's *Century* and McKerrow's *Printers' Dictionary* of 1910.

What is undeniable is that *STC* has been the major preoccupation of the Society, certainly while I was Secretary and afterwards. The correspondence file dwarfs all others; so does the bill for research and printing. Despite the magnitude of the ultimate achievement – and we still haven't finished – some of the supple-mentary volumes, such as the Printers' Index – it has probably had a baleful effect on our activities. We have really averted our eyes from Donald Wing's original work on the successor volumes to *STC* – though that much-loved figure was noted as a Society member when his work was recorded in *Studies in Retrospect*. The revision of Wing, largely undertaken at Yale, has received a great deal of help from individual members in this country, but it doesn't claim the same degree of bibliographical precision as Miss Pantzer's *STC* and will no doubt get published proportionately more quickly. The Society has however issued, as an Occasional Paper, Nelson and Seccombe's *Periodical Publications 1641–1700*[13] a category omitted from Wing.

It was in the days when Bill Jackson was at the height of his powers, and we were re-establishing cooperation between him and Ferguson, that the Society, feeling no doubt that *STC* was going well, and mindful of the fact that it had missed out on Wing, set up a small sub-committee on an 18th century *STC*. The sub-committee was chaired by the then President, Graham Pollard, and met ten times between December 1962 and May 1963. It produced a report saying in effect that the work could and should be done, on the basis of a pilot list – which of course is what ultimately happened. But the Society was soon hit by a series of crises – the death of W.A. Jackson in 1964 and the need to support financially the 1475–1640 *STC*, and the death of L.W. Hanson (who was both an 18th century bibliographer and, through the Bodleian, Jackson's principal supporter in Brit-ain), in 1966.

I used the report on the 18th century *STC* myself in a paper delivered in 1970[14] which I flatter myself kept the idea alive and again at the British Library-organised conference in June 1976 which finally got the *Eighteenth-Century Short-Title Catalogue* on the road. By then it had become a project which a relatively small members' Society could only influence and bless, though its members, British, European and American, took a leading part, and the initiative taken by the British Library was even more crucial than that it had taken in the original *STC* in 1918.

I have brought you almost up to date, because I wanted to follow through a concept which is essentially one of enumerative bibliography with standards of accuracy derived from material or physical bibliography. I believe that these standards have on the whole been applied in *STC* and *ESTC* and perhaps less rigidly in Wing. The justification for the Society's involvement in enumerative bibliography was set out by Greg; you had to know what books there were before you could study them.

There is one more concept that I'd like to follow through, that of 'special catalogues', because that like *STC*, was one of the threads that had to be picked up in the early 1960s. As early as 1903 the Society had declared itself willing to cooperate in publishing the catalogues of less known libraries, and that of Arch-bishop Marsh's Library in Dublin was produced in 1905 and that of Emmanuel College Cambridge in 1915. These two were numbered as a series, but it was to be a series of two only. But during the Second World War, Miss Margaret Hands, who had worked on the Inter-Collegiate Catalogue at Oxford, put a more ambi-tious plan to the Society, for a catalogue of early books in the Anglican Cathedral libraries of England and Wales. The plan was accepted; the Society supervised it, the Pilgrim Trust financed it, and Miss Hands began work at Worcester in 1944. The cold and discomfort can only be imagined, but Miss Hands had already endured the rigours of working in Oxford college libraries, and persevered until she had catalogued all but six of them (which included Canterbury, York and Durham). Then she left to get married. After her husband's death, this indomit-able lady returned to edit the catalogue and to add the contents of Carlisle Cathe-dral Library to it. The problem we were then faced with was to complete the work and publish the catalogue. Two developments were in the end to make this possible. One was the creation of new universities at Canterbury and York, which ensured the presence of concerned bibliographers and librarians in these cities, as there had been and still were, at Durham. The second development was the British Library Act. The Society pointed out in its evidence to the Dainton Committee on the National Library that by supporting the Cathedral Libraries Catalogue the society had performed a national function. The hint must have been taken, for under section 1.3(b) of the Act, the British Library could provide funds for the cataloguing of other libraries. The Cathedral project was one of the first beneficiaries of this enlightened clause; staff were recruited to catalogue the remaining libraries, the University of Kent, prompted by our member Dr David Shaw provided space and computer facilities, and the first volume[15] of the Cath-dral Libraries catalogue was published in 1984; the second will not be long delayed.

I promised to return to *Studies in Retrospect* and to F.S. Ferguson in particular. Ferguson's chapter, *English Books before 1640*, is exhaustive and very impressive (note by the way that there is nothing in *Studies* on English books from 1641–1700). It sums up the very great deal of work that had been done inside and outside the Bibliographical Society since its foundation and its being directed into the special field of British bibliography by Gordon Duff, Pollard, McKerrow and Greg, and how much had also been achieved by the indefatigable energy in examining documentary sources of figures like H.R. Plomer. Ferguson was also very clear about what he wanted to see; no doubt if he had been asked he would have said that the 1926 edition of *STC* was only an interim product, diverting the Society from a more distant goal. This goal included a chronological rearrangement of *STC*, to which he gave the title *Annals of Printing*. The nearest we have got to this so far has been a chronological card file, produced by the Folger Library, but the Society will provide a chronological index to the revised *STC*, and Mr Philip Rider has already indexed the second volume of this. Ferguson also hoped for a monograph on printers' ornaments and initials. He did himself have a long file of these mounted on cards, derived from tracings, photographs, illustrations from catalogues and, dare I say it, initials removed from imperfect books. This file passed to the British Museum on his death, and it was tidied up there and made available. He called also for revised printers' dictionaries, and finally mentioned a project of his own, a publication to replace Hazlitt's *Collations and Notes*. Standard collations of books had been a desideratum from the Society's earliest years; they would of course be a major preoccupation to an antiquarian bookseller. There was such a file among Ferguson's papers at the Museum and it has been suggested that the pursuit impeded Ferguson's collaboration in *STC*.

It has been said in the past, by me and others, that preoccupation with the admittedly bad printing of Elizabethan literature and in particular of the drama has distorted bibliographical studies in Britain. If I did say this, I now realise it was not true; if others said it, it was because they were making excuses for not having produced 'L'apparition du livre' or 'L'histoire de l'édition anglaise', and they should not have made such excuses. *Studies in Retrospect* does, however, make it clear how large Shakespearian and other textual studies then loomed among bibliographers, for F.P. Wilson's chapter is by far the longest. It is clear, however, that the direction of the Society had been settled *before* such events as Greg's demonstration of the dating of the Pavier quartos,[16] Pollard's *Shakespeare Folios and Quartos*[17] and his and Dover Wilson's challengingly titled paper 'What follows if some of the good quarto editions of Shakespeare's plays were printed from his autograph manuscripts'.[18] The length and magisterial quality of F.P. Wilson's chapter perhaps disguises the fact that the 'new bibliography' was at a watershed. For while the period surveyed was marked, for Wilson, by the Society, represented by its three most distinguished members, as 'the leader and inspirer of these studies', and while the decade of *Studies in Retrospect* also covered the issuing of the Society's most substantial publication, Greg's *Bibliography of the English Printed Drama to the Restoration*, the map of bibliographical studies was changing. The 'new bibliography' had become orthodoxy. The transfer of books, and in particular editions of Shakespeare, to the Huntington and Folger libraries, to Harvard and Yale, meant that textual bibliography was self-supporting in America and firmly established in the academic world there. This move was underlined by Charlton Hinman's *Printing and Proof Reading of the First Folio of Shakespeare*, 1963, based largely on the copies in the Folger Library, and by the founding of *Studies in Bibliography* under the inspiration of Professor Fredson Bowers in 1948. Typically, Hinan first published in *The Library* and only later in *Studies*. The dispersal of bibliography had begun; it was being dispersed into universities, and while you can certainly find articles, for example on compositor analysis, in *The Library*, this area of bibliography has largely disappeared from the Society's preoccupations. And I doubt whether Bowers's continuation of Greg beyond the Restoration, will, if that great and good man completes it, find a publisher in the Society.

It may indeed be thought that textual bibliography has learned its limitations; textual editors now know so much about the relations between quartos and folios that they cannot decide on the merits of their texts, and print both of them, as in the new Oxford Shakespeare.

But that was in the future, and F.P. Wilson's celebration of the triumph of the new bibliography overshadows everything else in *Studies in Retrospect*, and it was to become, with the support of Fredson Bowers, the dominant theme in bibliography for the next 20 years; it certainly seemed that way to me when as a newcomer to the British Museum I contributed a piece to *Library Trends* on 'Printed books to 1640' in 1959.[19]

It would be surprising if a certain loss of nerve had not been felt among textual bibliographers as a result of an article printed in *Studies in Bibliography* in 1969, entitled 'Printers of the Mind; some notes on bibliographical theories and printing house practices.'[20]

Set beside F.P. Wilson's article in *Studies in Retrospect* there is a distinctly apologetic note about the contributions of Harold Williams on the 18th Century; the Society had really shown very little interest in this period. He did however note the growing American involvement in 18th-century studies, without, I think, realising how much of it was connected with Yale University and the extraordinary impetus given to bibliographical and literary studies by the presence there of C.B. Tinker. When we were discussing the creation of an 18th century *STC* in the early 1970s, we were very conscious that the scholarship of this period had been retarded by the absence of bibliographical work, even of listing (of the kind with which Greg had begun). The great pioneer work of this kind was of course David Foxon's *English Verse 1701–1750, a catalogue of separately printed poems*, 1975, not a Society publication, but carried out by a prominent member who reported on his work to our meetings. Note that he did not call his work a bibliography; one of the greatest qualities of it is that he was able to balance bibliographical precision with economy of description and attention to literary content. And he finished the job.

The two other major contributions to *Studies in Retrospect* look forward to future bibliographical work in interestingly different ways. I do not know how

E.P. Goldschmidt got on with Walter Greg in life, but in these pages they clash, and I judge Greg the loser. This is Greg;

'... book-binding, another subject that has particularly appealed to the dilettante. Binding is intimately concerned with the preservation of books, and should therefore be a quite important concern of the bibliographer. But the decoration of bindings is either a particular department of decorative leatherwork in general – no doubt a subject of great interest in its own way – or else, if it takes the form of armorial bearings and the like, is concerned with ownership and what collectors and their purveyors like to call "association" ... '.[21]

Now Goldschmidt;

The study of old bookbindings is a sideline of the main course of bibliographical research ... Bibliography proper might be compared to Political or Constitutional History, the History of Bookbinding to the History of Costume. A humble auxiliary discipline, rather childish to some, attractive others, not entirely useless and undoubtedly innocuous'.[22]

Goldschmidt's diffidence is deceptive. He goes on to trace the history of bookbinding studies from the Society's earliest years; 'when our Society was founded we were in the midst of the "aesthetic" period of Arts and Crafts, of the cult of Beauty and Good Taste'. Omitting to say that this was no doubt the period when Greg's attitudes were formed, he traced binding studies through the strictly utilitarian (though beautifully printed) works of Strickland Gibson and G.J. Gray on the bindings of Oxford and Cambridge, the work of Gordon Duff (documented in his sale catalogue) and G.D. Hobson. Binding studies for Goldschmidt are analogous to other forms of bibliography, using historical documentation and the precise recording of blocks, rolls and individual tools. Although not represented, except in the earliest days, by actual monographs, work of this kind has regularly formed part of the Society's programme; a very large part in fact, when we remember the papers given by J.B. Oldham, Graham Pollard, A.R.A. Hobson and H.M. Nixon. Perhaps for technical reasons much of the work has found outside publishers – for example. Howard Nixon's and later Mirjam Foot's long series of contributions to the *Book Collector*.

Michael Sadleir's contribution to *Studies in Retrospect* has exceptional interest. In the first place, as he acknowledged, he was dealing with something that the Society had all but ignored – though he detected an increasing American interest in the 19th century. Secondly, Sadleir, writing nearly 10 years after the event, was able to regard the T.J. Wise disaster dispassionately in a way that A.W. Pollard could not. I quote Pollard to McKerrow on the subject of the Society's Gold Medal, writing in February 1935;

But though I take your view as to the improbability of his authorship of the bad booklets it is discreditable to his acumen as a bibliographer if he failed to suspect them when so many passed through his hands and he must take the responsibility for the chief share in putting them on the market. With all my affection for him I think he must be regarded as out of the running.

But as Sadleir saw, Wise's influence on the bibliophily and bibliography of the 19th century could not be ignored; indeed, Simon Nowell-Smith returned to it in his Presidential Address in 1963. By that time Wise had been denounced to the Society over which he had once presided, as a thief, and details of his dishonest bookselling were to follow.

To return to Sadleir, however. It is in this article, I believe, that we can detect concerns approximating to what we now call 'book history'. Sadleir had achieved a then-unrivalled eminence as a collector of 19th-century books, but he was also an author and a publisher, and he appears in these pages as an advocate of publishing history, giving high praise to those bibliographers who had gone beyond the mere description of books. I select only one example of this wider awareness;

The bibliographer may, therefore, be called upon to show knowledge or understanding of the relationship between author and publisher; the type of contract usual at any period . . . the fashion for part issue merging into that for magazine serial; the processes of book manufacture – paper, typography, illustration, binding and end-papers – in vogue at different times; the machinery of sale by publisher to wholesaler, retailer and circulating library, involving trade terms and other technicalities; the sequence of 'secondary' and of cheaper editions and their physical qualities; the publisher-jobber who sold other firms' sheets over his own imprint; the gradual development of the remainder as we understand it to-day.

'This is a large order' says Sadleir,[23] and with that I end my quotation and my cursory overview of *Studies in Retrospect. Studies* reveals a small intimate bibliographical world, where everyone knew everyone else, where Pollard met McKerrow to talk about the Wise affair on the steps of the British Museum, wondering in his honourable confusion whether they could somehow give a medal to the book (the *Enquiry*) and to Wise as well. Graham Pollard told me that he only met Wise twice. Predictably neither meeting was a success.

In a way the Society's success diminished its role. I have already noted how the 'new bibliography' was to harden into an orthodoxy, as a subject of academic study in Britain and even more in the United States. W.A. Copinger's vision of bibliographical societies in every major city was to become a reality, and there are in Britain alone at least 12 sister-societies to that of London, plus two groups of the Library Association (Rare Books and Library History). The reasons for this dramatic diffusion are not far to seek, for they lie with the founding of more universities (all the societies are in university cities) and with the moving forward in time of bibliographical studies. Many of the societies are engaged in studies of the local book trade, which spread rapidly outside London, Oxford and Cambridge with the lapse of the Licensing Act in 1695.

Setting aside the proliferation of bibliographical societies in America (and the bibliographical apostolate of Terry Belanger from Columbia University) in Australia and New Zealand and doubtless elsewhere, there are two specialised areas in which the Society has conceded its rights. These are occupied by the Printing Historical Society and its *Journal* founded in 1965 and *Publishing History* which was first issued in 1977. The *Book Collector* also, though its constituency is more strictly bibliophilic often prints articles which could equally well appear in *The Library*.

It was my privilege that the first President of the Society that I served with as Secretary was Graham Pollard. I don't think it was simply *because* he was the first that I nailed my bibliographical colours to his mast in the intention that if I had any influence, I would make it Pollard's kind of Bibliographical Society. Although the diffusion of bibliographical effort had begun, it had not gone so far as it was to go; but he could see it happening and tried to define a role for the Society.[22] He presided, as I have already remarked, over the Sub-Committee that met 10 times and reported in 1963 on the feasibility of an 18th-century *STC*. He set up a Programme Sub-Committee, now lapsed, which was to approach interesting speakers and ask them for papers, rather than wait for the (occasionally embarrassing) offer. He set up a Publications Sub-Committee and drew up a policy statement on publications which suggested the commissioning of editions of documents of bibliographical importance, including facsimiles. One product of this was to be an edition of Liber A of the Stationers' Company, of which he procured a photocopy and a transcript, intending to edit it himself. It was he who suggested the publishing of a facsimile edition of the Bowyer ledgers, a project which under the editorship of Keith Maslen and the joint auspices of the Society and the Bibliographical Society of America, is now coming to fruition. Graham also initiated a series of evening discussion meetings. These tended to be solo performances, but they were all the better for that.

This is not of course to disparage initiatives taken by other Presidents – one thinks of Walter Oakeshott's financial campaign for *STC*, Anthony Hobson's powerful and successful advocacy of cathedral libraries and Nicolas Barker's attention to the financing of publications and to the management of *STC* – but Graham Pollard for me remains the President who tried to define a role for the Society, and influences its activities long after his death.

The pioneers of the Bibliographical Society have a proud record of achievement in the study of the book, both manuscript and printed, in Britain and abroad, for Anglo-American bibliography has been one of our most successful joint exports. One reason for the success has been the variety of interests involved, those of literary scholars, antiquarian booksellers, librarians, bibliophiles and plain inquisitive amateurs. To go back to *Studies in Retrospect* for a moment, what an enormous amount F.S. Ferguson the antiquarian bookseller knew about the people who printed books in England (and Scotland) before 1640; how comprehensively had the publisher Michael Sadleir thought about the processes, physical, intellectual and commercial, which brought about the artefacts he described in his *XIX Century Fiction*. We know, thanks to innumerable authors of monographs and contributors to *The Library* and other journals, a very great deal about the book in Britain, as much, I should hazard a guess, as the authors of *L'Apparition du livre* knew about the book in France and much more than they knew about other people's books. John Feather pointed out in an address to the Society nearly 10 years ago and published in 1980,[25] that what we know is largely bibliocentric, as opposed to the knowledge based on documentary sources which has proved so valuable in France.

What then is the Society, any Society *for*? Clearly it isn't quite like a committee, though it may express itself by means of one. Ours was a voluntary grouping for which W.A. Copinger (and Sir John McAlister) perceived the need, a grouping of people who were interested in books in a historical way. Their interests were badly focussed at first, but the focus was sharpened by A.W. Pollard, Greg and McKerrow in such a way that the concerns of scholars of literature, antiquarian booksellers, collectors and the national libraries (particularly the British Museum) were concentrated upon the completion of a definitive record of the book in Britain, and upon the study of books outside Britain, which we could do because, practising a kind of beneficent cultural imperialism we had acquired other people's books as historically important to us.

With *STC* behind it, and its centenary coming up, the Bibliographical Society needs to sharpen its focus again. D.F. McKenzie has recently reminded us in his Panizzi lectures that we are far from exhausting the meaning of bibliography and that the material of bibliography has, as Greg foresaw it more than 40 years ago, moved far beyond signs made upon paper with movable types. I'm reasonably certain that McKenzie was nudging the British Library rather hard about its duties when it moves into its new building. I'm not sure that was wholly understood, but the fact remains that the health of our national library and the health of bibliography are inextricably linked.

There is, however an area where the Bibliographical Society does not need to move too far from its traditional concerns, can capitalise upon the knowledge it has accumulated in its *Transactions* and its publications and resume its pioneering. Most of you will know that a project for the History of the Book in Britain – the phrase is here in capital letters, having previously in this paper been in lower case – has now reached an advanced stage of planning. Very few of the topics listed for the earlier volumes will be strange to readers of *The Library*, though their place in a larger design will certainly be unfamiliar. The outline submitted to funding bodies considers 'the relations of the project to external interested parties (such as the short-title catalogues, national and university libraries, the Bibliographical Society, and the Book Trade History Group, and similar projects in other countries'. It looks to the publication of the research generated by the project, but not publishable within the span of six volumes; and foresees a need for the material within the six volumes to be supplemented by specialist articles, surveys and monographs.

I should like to put this in a slightly different way, because projectors are optimistic people, and the volumes of the History will probably be a long time in compiling. Rather, the material in the published volumes will need to be digested *from* specialist articles and surveys.

This is surely where societies like ours come in; they may have to change their habits a little, but I should like to see them thinking now about the gaps in knowledge and commissioning the papers and studies upon which the definitive books will be based. But I hope also that we won't simply become little Englanders, because we still have a lot to say, and a lot to learn about books from abroad.

References

 1. A.W. Pollard, 'Our twenty-first birthday', *Transactions of the Bibliographical Society*, 13, 1916, 9–27.
 2. W.A. Copinger, 'Inaugural address'. *Tr. Bib. Soc*, 1, 1893, pp.31–59.
 3. Henry B. Wheatley, 'The present condition of English Bibliography, and suggestions for its future', *Tr. Bib. Soc*, 1, 1893, pp.61–90.
 4. *Studies in Retrospect*, p.4.
 5. D.F. McKenzie, *Bibliography and the sociology of texts* (London, British Library, 1986).
 6. A.W. Pollard and W.W. Greg, 'Some points in bibliographical descriptions', *Tr. Bib. Soc*, 9, 1908, pp.31–52.
 7. F. Madan, 'Digressive bibliography', *Tr. Bib. Soc*, 9, 1908, pp.53–65.
 8. See above, n.1.
 9. F. Madan, 'Edward Gordon Duff (1863–1924),' '*The Library*, 4th ser., 5, 1925, pp.264–66.
10. A.W. Pollard to R.B. McKerrow, 4 and 6 Feb. 1935. The letters are in the Society's archives.
11. 'Journal', *Tr. Bib. Soc*, 15, 1920, pp.5–7.
12. A.W. Pollard, 'The Short-Title Catalogue of English Books, 1501–1640', *Tr. Bib. Soc*, 15, 1920, pp.142–48.
13. C. Nelson and M. Seccombe, *Periodical publications 1641–1700: a survey with illustrations* (London, Bibliographical Society, 1986).
14. R.J. Roberts, 'Towards a short-title catalogue of English eighteenth century books', *Jnl of Librarianship*, 3, 1970, pp.246–62.
15. Margaret S.G. McLeod, *The Cathedral Libraries catalogue: books printed before 1701 in the libraries of the Anglican cathedrals of England and Wales*, (London: the British Library; the Bibliographical Society, 1984).
16. W.W. Greg, 'On certain false dates in Shakespearian quartos', *The Library*, new ser. 9, 1908, pp.113–31 and 381–409.
17. A.W. Pollard, *Shakespeare folios and quartos*. (London, Metheun, 1909).
18. A.W. Pollard and J. Dover Wilson, 'What follows if some of the good quarto editions of Shakespeare's plays were printed from his autograph manuscripts', *Tr. Bib. Soc*, 15, 1920, pp.136–39.
19. Julian Roberts, 'Printed books to 1640', *Library Trends*, 1959, pp.517–36.
20. D.F. McKenzie, 'Printers of the mind: some notes on bibliographical theories and printing-house pratices', *Studies in Bibliography*, 22, 1969, pp.1–75.
21. *Studies in Retrospect*, 26.
22. *Studies in Retrospect*, 175.
23. *Studies in Retrospect*, 154.
24. The lack of direction in the Society's affairs was the subject of correspondence between Pollard and John Johnson as early as 1939, and Pollard advocated sub-committees as a means of devolving the administration of the Society from the then Honorary Secretary, R.B. McKerrow, onto others. (Bodleian Library MSS Pollard 394, fol.45–49 and 395, 1–33 and 56–9.)
25. John Feather, 'Cross Channel currents: historical bibliography and "L'Histoire du livre"', *The Library*, 6th ser, 2, 1980, pp.1–15.

Discussion following the paper

Contributors – Gwyn Walters, Don McKenzie, Tom Birrell, Charles Rivington, Tony Lister, Peter Stockham, Michael Harris, Mirjam Foot, Michael Turner, Michael Winship, Robin Myers.

Concerning the mystery surrounding the personality of Gordon Duff, Julian Roberts suggested that his omission from the *DNB* might have been because of his intemperate habits. Don McKenzie expressed interest in him, pointing out that Stanley Morison had put the case for Duff. It was an abrupt and laconic correspondence, such a vast accumulation of postcards, letters and little notes etc, that it would be an impossible task to work on it. Don McKenzie had once been asked to go to the Huntington by Bill Jackson, but he couldn't. Asked if the Huntington had the Duff letters, Don McKenzie said they had not. Tom Birrell remarked on Duff's seeming vendetta with Cyril Davenport for when *English Heraldic Book Stamps* was published (1909) Duff commented that 'this is the most worthless book ever'. Another famous Duff remark was; 'when a woman gets her hands on a library, the first thing she does is sell it'. A question about the magic significance of the date 1640, brought suggestions that it was owing to the date of commencement of the Thomason Tracts, and the enormous increase in the amount of publishing after 1640. The *STC*, the Society's dictionaries of printers, and Bullen's British Museum catalogue compiled (1880s) all take 1640 as their starting or finishing date. Asked about H.R. Plomer who seemed a nebulous personality, Julian Roberts thought the others looked down on him because he wasn't a member of the BM staff, and regarded him as a slightly eccentric errand boy; he had a book business which collapsed and he picked up work here and there. He liked to run around and look in archives; but the dictionaries he edited for the Society are still good and useful.

Michael Harris next asked about the Society's policy on recruitment, pointing out how few historians were members. Mirjam Foot explained that they had once done a vast recruitment mailing, at enormous cost to the Society, and it brought in 10 new members – from Germany and Japan.

There was some discussion on the Anglo-Saxon concentration on descriptive, analytical and textual bibliography, and all agreed that we had done far more than other countries even though none of the great names – Greg, A.W. Pollard and Cyprian Blagden were specified – were in the least concerned with 'l'histoire du livre', but concentrated on textual criticism and editing, with a strong emphasis, in *Studies in Retrospect*, on pre-1640 English books. Mirjam Foot raised the question of a clash of personalities with Greg and E.P. Goldschmidt which she thought could have been part of the reason that Greg discounted the importance of binding in bibliography which could have been one of his strongest arguments. Graham Pollard was the first to understand the importance of binding structure but even he never put his argument for it on paper. Binding structure was the foundation stone for bibliography. Julian Roberts agreed that Greg's approach was narrow, he was only concerned with text, the marks on the paper.

Oxford books on Bibliography

ESTHER POTTER

NOWADAYS we tend to think of John Johnson, not as the editor of Greek papyri, nor even as one of the finest Printers to the University of Oxford, but as the far-seeing creator of the John Johnson collection of ephemeral printing, now in the Bodleian Library. But at the beginning he saw himself as a scholar (as indeed he was) rather than a collector. When circumstances diverted him from Egyptian excavation to publishing he used his spare time and remarkable energies to explore the unrivalled archives of the Oxford University Press, and, with the help of his friend Strickland Gibson, those of the University and the Bodleian Library. He was also collecting all the records he could lay hands on to illustrate the history of printing and bookselling. His aim was to create an archive which would be used to write the history of the book trade, and by the beginning of 1932 he was making plans for publishing some of his material.[1]

Up to January of 1932 he was assembling a miscellany volume of articles illustrating facets of the book trade. One of his collaborators was Stanley Morison who wrote on New Year's Day, 1932: 'I shall be quite interested to contribute further material to an enlarged volume'. Johnson replied: 'I had also a wild idea that we might rope in young Pollard of Birrell & Garnett to write the head and tail of the chapter on the Auctioneer. The rest I am doing here as a verse translation of Smalridge's *Auctio Davisiana* with all the allusions modernised.[2] I have got the best Plautine scholar in the world on it.' Dr Percy Simpson, a Shakespeare scholar and editor of Ben Johnson, suggested an expanded version of his paper on proof correcting, which had been printed in the *Proceedings* of the Oxford Bibliographical Society for 1927,[3] and also an article on pirate printing. Graham Pollard had suggested printing the very few surviving 17th-century lists of the charges for trade bookbinding agreed between the London booksellers and binders.

An important part of the volume was to be a version of the paper on 'Proposals' that Johnson had read to the Double Crown Club on November 5th 1931. (That was when he first met Graham Pollard who was there as the guest of the publisher Michael Sadleir of Constable & Co.) Proposals are prospectuses for books to be published by subscription and Johnson had a substantial collection of them.[4] He was re-arranging and amplifying his paper at the behest of Humphrey Milford, Publisher to the Oxford University Press, who wanted a Monograph. 'Monograph' was coming in at the Press as a useful alternative to 'essay', 'paper', 'study' and such like.

By February 1932 Johnson's plans had changed. After consulting Strickland Gibson and Theodore Besterman, another of his collaborators, he wrote to Stanley Morison: 'I have a better idea ... Instead of a loosely-knit volume of a Miscellany I plan a little series of Monographs to make accessible as quickly as can be whatever documents I may have, or may have accessible, to illustrate the history of book making. Your disquisition on the Fell types would make one of these little Monographs, but I want to add to it all the letters and documents which exist in the archives or in the Bodleian. Oh Morison: say you approve. For the moment I brim with ideas and do not want to be discouraged.'[5] The following day the chief collaborators met for dinner in London. Johnson, Morison, Theodore Besterman and Pollard were there, and they concluded their discussion as they saw Johnson off on his train back to Oxford. Strickland Gibson, an essential partner in this enterprise, was not with them but Johnson reported to him the next day: 'Things took shape nicely late last night on the platform at Paddington Station. It was so chilly that business leapt forward quickly. Stanley Morison joins the gang and contributes the monograph on the Fell Types. Young Pollard of Birrell and Garnett will do binding prices of two centuries. You will do the Paper...'[6]

Morison confirmed his approval the day after: ' "Oxford Studies in English Book Production" is a marvellously good idea'. An editorial board was formed of John Johnson, Strickland Gibson, Stanley Morison and Theodore Besterman. Besterman, then quite a young man, was a little diffident about his place in such distinguished company, but Johnson wrote reassuringly: 'you give me that sense of bibliographical confidence most necessary to my stumbling steps'. It is true that Besterman's main preoccupation at this time was psychical research, but he also lectured on bibliography to the University of London's School of Librarianship. Of the other editors, Strickland Gibson was the founder of the Oxford Bibliographical Society and a highly respected bibliographer. Dr Chapman wrote in 1935 that descriptive bibliography, 'which was born in the British Museum under [A.W.] Pollard and Co. has now virtually migrated to Oxford, and this is perhaps due above all to Gibson'. Morison had an established reputation as a typographer and was typographical adviser to the Cambridge University Press and to the Monotype Corporation. Meetings of the editorial board took the form of fortnightly suppers in London at which they passed on to each other the discoveries they had made. By March they had co-opted Graham Pollard and it is these five who supervised the volumes that were eventually published.

Discussion of a title for the series, which was not finalised until the first volumes were published in 1935, uncovered some misconceptions. Would a series of pamphlets of different sizes and shapes really make much impact? But this was not what John Johnson envisaged. He had in mind a uniform series of volumes, imperial octavo in size in order to give a large page for collotype illustrations, and running to an average of 96 pages. (In the event they averaged about double that length.) Johnson did not want to have the word 'bibliography' in the title: he was anxious to avoid any direct challenge of Michael Sadleir's 'Bibliographia' series which Constable had recently started. Morison thought the word 'Oxford' ought to appear.

In between the convivial meetings in London letters flew back and forth. It was not unusual for John Johnson to write two or even three letters to the same person in one day. He was busy consulting his many academic friends about potential talent – Professor David Nichol Smith was a close confidant. Professor Cesare Foligno, a Clarendon Press author, was looking on Johnson's behalf for someone to write on early trade relations between publisher, author, bookseller and paper maker in Italy during the first 100 or 150 years of printing. Johnson had not succeeded in enlisting for this subject the obvious person – Victor Scholderer, then a deputy keeper in the Department of Printed Books in the British Museum and a noted incunabulist. Johnson was also looking at the books he had planned to write himself from the material he had collected. Booksellers' margins, authors' terms, an edition of the first minute book of the Delegates of the Oxford Press as well as the Proposals on which he had lectured to the Double Crown Club were all on his list. But he had a full-time and exacting job as University Printer which did not leave much spare time for academic research as well as building up and arranging his collection of ephemeral printing. He wanted to write a good deal himself, but he was a realist. So when he found a good man for a subject he had been working on he handed over his file and followed it up with more material as he discovered it.

Some of the books planned for the Series arose from work already on the stocks – Morison's notes on the Fell types, for example, and Percy Simpson's article on proof correcting. Turner Berry, librarian of the St Bride Institute, and A.F. Johnson of the British Museum were compiling a list of type specimens, and Johnson's own work on the Delegates' minute book seems to have been well advanced. Some were new ideas. 'I should love a volume on the development of valentines' he wrote to Morison, 'or perhaps' he went on 'a little sub series called jobbing printing ... I wonder whether young Simon Nowell Smith (he is an able writer) might not be roped in'. Some subjects arose from chance discoveries and encounters. Johnson was actively searching for book trade records. He used to go to London, usually on a Thursday, and hunt through the debris in booksellers' basements. 'I drifted up to Town yesterday', he wrote to Theodore Besterman, 'and had incredible luck in dropping on a whole dossier of Cadell & Davies correspondence ... all for a few shillings.' A few days later a short monograph by Besterman on Cadell & Davies was added to the programme. Professor C.R. Cheney had met an old acquaintance, L.W. Hanson, who worked in the Department of Printed Books of the British Museum and who was interested in the relations of the Government to the Press in the 18th century. Hanson knew of some records of a Halifax bookbinder[7] and Professor Cheney thought Johnson might like to ask him about them. Johnson went to see Hanson but what he came away with was not the archives of Edwards of Halifax but a promise to write up Government and the Press as a Monograph.

By the end of March there were about 20 volumes in prospect. Besterman was to contribute also the evolution of subject catalogues, and he tried out part of his monograph in the form of a lecture at University College, London in November 1932. By the time it was finished the title had become 'The beginnings of systematic bibliography'; it was a preliminary to his *World Bibliography of Bibliographies*. Percy Simpson promised to shape his proof correcting 'next term'. Piracy must wait he said: he was deep in *Volpone*. Simpson had been working on the definitive edition of Ben Jonson since 1903; four volumes had so far been published and the eleventh and last volume did not appear until 1952. So Sir Charles Firth warned Johnson not to lead Simpson away from Ben Jonson, and piracy waited until 1946 when Percy Simpson read a paper to the Oxford Bibliographical Society.[8] Graham Pollard's reprint of the bookbinding price lists was developing into a study of the structure and economics of the wholesale trade in bookbinding on the lines of an article he had written for *The Times Literary Supplement* with some documents.[9] Johnson considered a history of shorthand. He had found, while he was excavating in Egypt just before the First World War, portions of a Greek manual on shorthand; but he thought the Egyptian Exploration Society might take that over, and his fellow editors did not think it would fit well into the Series. Type design featured prominently in the scheme. Johnson was planning to collaborate with Sidney Squires, typographer at the Oxford Press, Stanley Morison and Strickland Gibson in a monograph on Nicholas Nicholls, typefounder of London, who was one of the earliest typefounders to supply the press in Oxford. He provided a roman and italic fount for printing the 1674 catalogue of the Bodleian. The subject of this monograph was soon expanded to 'The earliest printing types of Oxford University 1637–1667'.

It seems to have been understood about this time that the principal contributors, while working in their main field, would keep an eye open for material on, as it were, a subsidiary subject. Hanson was looking at 'the mechanism of the magazine (and annual) to include the Annual Register &c. but not the newspaper'. Besterman took 'publicity' as his background job. Johnson offered Morison some exhibits if he was going to do something on Postal History. In fact this idea was quite plausible. The postal services were vital in the early days for the gathering of news and for the distribution of newspapers and Morison had looked at them when he was preparing his Sandars lectures on *The English Newspaper*. He was now vainly trying to find time to write the early history of the Post Office.[10]

In a letter to Milford early in June, Johnson said that he had enough material collected to form the basis of an admirable monograph on 'authors' terms'. But who would do it? John Sparrow was too full. He dare not ask Michael Sadleir. After failing to persuade Milford to take it on he supposed he would have to do it himself. Johnson would probably have liked to do it himself. He was complaining to Milford that he hadn't enough spare time for his own research, and that he couldn't get the papers written that he wanted. He had to make do with what he could get. What he had got so far was the complete manuscript of the Berry and Johnson bibliography of type specimens and a promise from Percy Simpson to deliver 'Proof correcting through the centuries' by the beginning of August.[11] Strickland Gibson had collected a good deal of the material for the volume on paper and had started to write. Laurence Hanson was working away steadily at Government and the Press.

From the beginning it had been assumed that the monographs would be published by Humphrey Milford in London; but now Milford was concerned lest Dr

R.W. Chapman, Secretary to the Delegates of the Press and thus Publisher in Oxford, might be offended if the Series, which were obviously Clarendon Press type books, appeared with Milford's London imprint. The theory was that the Clarendon Press in Oxford published works of scholarship and the Oxford University Press in London those of general interest; but the distinction was becoming increasingly blurred. Music and medicine, for example had been tacitly handed over to London. But the Monographs were already being talked about far and wide (Philip Hofer had indeed written to say the New York Public Library would subscribe to every one) and what was Milford to say to the Delegates if they asked: 'as they naturally may in these unprofitmaking times why such important and expensive works are planned and carried out without their knowledge.' Milford would have been happier if he could at least let Chapman know officially about the Monographs. The Delegates were aware of what was being published in Oxford but the activities of the London business rarely came to their notice. Johnson replied that it was the custom for officials at Oxford to avoid the personal publicity that would accrue from publishing in Oxford and to carry their wares to London: and in any case that Graham Pollard, the most active of the general editors, could in no way work with Chapman. They were utterly different sorts of bibliographers and neither would understand the other.[12]

Milford accepted this and Johnson turned to consider a suggestion from A.F. Johnson for printing a catalogue he had prepared of 'London newspapers in the British Museum'. The only one of Johnson's editorial colleagues who was in favour of it was Morison. It was thought that the holdings of a single library was too narrow a field and the English faculty in Oxford (well represented among the Delegates) would not like the omission of literary periodicals. And so it was rejected. Among the early titles considered were the typography of playbills, by Morison, and the booksellers of cheap plays, by Pollard. Jan van Krimpen was to compile a bibliography of the type specimen books of Holland as a companion to the Berry and Johnson book.

In September 1932 Johnson received Besterman's manuscript of the beginnings of systematic bibliography and circulated it to the other editors for comment. He was delighted with the detailed and constructive criticisms he received from Pollard and passed them on to Besterman with his own demand for an extra chapter to carry the story through the 17th century. Besterman was the most amenable of Johnson's authors. When he had recovered from the shock of receiving Pollard's remarks in the characteristically forthright form in which they had been sent to Johnson (Pollard had written on the assumption that Johnson would pass on only the gist of what he said and not his *ipsissima verba*) he went away and rewrote his monograph and added the extra chapter that Johnson wanted.[13]

Meanwhile the bibliography of type specimens was being set up in type. By December 1932 the proofs were back for revise and the collotypes settled. Now this book was not published until 1935; nor were any of the others in the series. What happened in the interim was known in the Press as 'The Rumpus'.[14] Professor Hugh Last was appointed a Delegate of the Press and a member of the Finance Committee in 1932 and started a searching investigation into the reasons for poor profitability. One might have supposed that there was no need to look beyond the great depression that had started in 1929; and the implication of inefficiency did nothing for the morale of the officers of the Press who had really done very well in the circumstances. But with a self-appointed management consultant at large, this was no time to launch a series that was expensive to produce (all those collotypes!) and was not likely to sell in large numbers.

So Milford and Johnson bided their time but the editorial work went on with undiminished enthusiasm. Johnson wanted Pollard to collaborate with him on what he called 'a modest chrestomathy of the principal documents'. This was established in the programme with the title 'Select Documents of the Bookselling Trade', and was generally referred to as the Chrestomathy, not to be confused with the original miscellany volume to which the same term was sometimes applied. 'Chrestomathy' is defined by the *Shorter Oxford Dictionary* as 'collection of choice passages', and the intention was to print in this volume a transcript of original documents which were important sources for the history of the book trade down to 1830 with notes by Pollard on their significance. Milford agreed that it was a very good idea and the Chrestomathy got going in a burst of enthusiasm. 'I grow more and more thrilled by the Select Documents idea,' Johnson wrote to Pollard in December 1932, 'and Strickland Gibson agrees that it must come out under your name; we shall be your willing slaves and shall do whatever you tell us to do.' Many of the documents that Johnson had assembled on book trade economics were candidates for this volume. Authors' terms were included and the *Auctio Davisiana*. Besterman was asked to arrange for photostats to be made of a stack of book trade letters in the Public Record Office. Pollard found others in the archives of the Stationers' Company. The documents were transcribed – I think by Gibson – and copied by Johnson's typist. By the middle of 1933 the essential material had grown so much that Pollard thought two volumes would be needed. Johnson invited him to lunch with Milford to discuss it. Milford's verdict was: 'I think we must, in spite of bad present trade and worse to follow, go for the larger scheme.'

Another subject that was considered about the same time was the trade in school books, on which Johnson had some material. He was impressed by Pollard's ability to prepare a detailed outline for a volume on many book trade subjects and in December 1932 he wrote: 'I wonder whether you can draw up one of your inimitable conspectuses for this purpose too, so that we can get the gang to work in search of facts'. For once Pollard declined on the grounds that he didn't know enough about the subject. Johnson did not give up. A couple of months later he had persuaded John Butt to take it on. He was then lecturer in English at Bedford College, London, but had earlier been assistant librarian in the English School in Oxford when Percy Simpson was librarian.

In March 1933 Johnson, Morison and Pollard were thinking about the Berry and Johnson type specimen book. There was a long standing theory at the Press that an introduction by a distinguished personality sold a book and Pollard agreed that nothing else would sell this one. This raised two questions. Would Morison write the Introduction and would the authors accept it if he did? Pollard had a special interest in type specimens – the famous Birrell and Garnett catalogue of type specimens had come out in 1928. He provided Morison with an outline of his introduction in the hope that, like the piece of grit in the oyster, it would provoke Morison into doing something better himself. It did! In the end Johnson had to assert his authority as publisher with the authors. 'Of course I am delighted that Mr Morison has promised to write an introduction', replied Turner Berry. A.F. Johnson's answer was summarised as 'Johnson writes not too grudgingly'. The introduction turned out to be an important essay on the history of type design. Morison's name appeared on the title page, and internal notes in the Press tended to refer to the work as 'Morison' rather than 'Berry and Johnson'. The book then went into cold storage 'waiting for the world to revive' as Johnson said.

Johnson had Percy Simpson's manuscript of 'Proof-reading' early in 1934, followed, of course, by Pollard's criticisms. This time the author was delighted with them: his thanks prompted further suggestions and a lively correspondence followed. Hanson's manuscript was in Johnson's hands by the end of May, and in July arrived a volume by Frank Isaac entitled *English printers' types of the sixteenth century*. Colonel Isaac had been analysing early English types for A.W. Pollard in the British Museum, and two volumes by him had been published by the Bibliographical Society. Pollard was unhappy with the book, not least because he had encouraged Johnson to accept it when the idea was first suggested. He was reluctant to discuss the book with Isaac because he did not expect him to welcome criticism from a much younger man. But Isaac did accept some of his criticisms and amended his text. Morison declined to write an introduction; he said he was too busy with the history of *The Times*. He grumbled that, because of the separation of printed books and manuscripts in the British Museum, Isaac knew nothing of palaeography and all he could do for him was to recommend a couple of books on the subject. It was important, he went on, that Oxford should be seen to publish works of real scholarship and not like the stuff they turned out in London. A short introduction was provided by A.W. Pollard who had encouraged the work from the start.

The Oxford Press recorded rather better profit figures for the financial year 1933–34, and in September 1934 Strickland Gibson wrote to Pollard triumphantly: 'The Monographs are moving'. There was a flurry of consultation about a general title for the series. They settled on 'Oxford Books on Bibliography', Pollard and Johnson began drafting prospectuses for the individual books and also a general prospectus for the series in which they explained: 'The object, then, of the present series is to publish studies in the past practice of all occupations which affect the making and distribution of books. It will not include lists of the works of individual authors or on particular subjects; and, conscious that the analytical investigation of books is encouraged elsewhere, this series will be confined to studies in the material upon which such work must ultimately rest.'

The first three volumes were issued in 1935 at intervals of two or three months. Johnson was set on making Percy Simpson's *Proof-reading* the first of the series. Johnson had spent 10 years on the publishing side of the Clarendon Press before becoming Printer, and he recognised that this was the volume to make the most impact. Milford called it 'a wonderful book' and Morison's verdict was 'a much more impressive affair than I had anticipated': that, from Morison, was high praise. Five hundred copies had been printed with the title *Proof-reading in the sixteenth, seventeenth and eighteenth centuries*. It was, as planned, on imperial octavo paper with 17 collotype plates. The price was 45 shillings. Johnson had been at pains to get a soft flexible paper. *The Times*, in a lyrical moment, called it 'a book in which the author and the printer have joined to produce a harmony of learning and beauty'. It was in a quarter binding of pinkish fawn boards with a dark blue cloth spine and a dust wrapper of the same pinkish fawn paper. The title of the series, *Oxford Books on Bibliography*, appears prominently on the dust wrapper along with extracts from the prospectus; but unless you have a copy with a dust wrapper there is nothing in the volume itself to tell you about the series.

The future of the series depended a good deal on how this volume was received. By Christmas it had been reviewed in a dozen English periodicals and several continental ones. *The Times Literary Supplement*[15] devoted most of the first two pages of its issue of 4 April to a long review which welcomed the series and praised the book, noting the accuracy of the printing and the high quality of the collotypes. Johnson was working hard, and with notable success, to raise the standard of printing in Oxford; and the handsome production of this and other volumes in the series was often noted, sometimes with a wry comment on the high price. There was a less enthusiastic review in *The Library*[16] by Dr R.B. McKerrow, its editor and Secretary of the Bibliographical Society. He made only a passing reference to the introduction of an important new bibliographical series, which can probably be ascribed to McKerrow's poor health rather than malice, because he had offered Johnson free insertion in *The Library* on the grounds that *The Library* existed to encourage bibliography.

Proof-reading was followed by the *Catalogue of specimens of printing types by English and Scottish printers and founders, 1665–1830* by W. Turner Berry and A.F. Johnson, with an Introduction by Stanley Morison. The price was 42 shillings. The review in *The Times Literary Supplement*[17] was approving and well-informed, which was not surprising since it was written by Pollard; but when David Thomas' article appeared in *The Library* in 1936 it was decidedly unfavourable.[18] Pollard was indignant and A.F. Johnson wrote to *The Library* defending and praising Morison's introduction.[19] And when Morison was told that W.W. Greg was doing a very critical review of Percy Simpson's *Proof-reading* for the *Review of English Studies*, he and Pollard were convinced that this was an attempt by the London bibliographical establishment to discredit the Oxford venture. John Johnson took it more calmly. 'In spite of everything the series isn't doing too badly' he said. In fact all this was a false alarm because Dr Greg's article in the *Review of English Studies*, although it made some criticisms, pointed out at length the importance and value of *Proof-reading*.[20] Theodore Besterman's *Beginnings of systematic bibliography* appeared in the autumn of 1935. The editors must have been pleased by the TLS review of it which referred to the 'newly but firmly established Oxford Books on Bibliography'.[21]

The next two volumes were published early in 1936 together with a second, revised edition of *The beginnings of systematic bibliography*. Frank Isaac's *English printers' types of the sixteenth century* appeared at the beginning of the year. Johnson had not been put off by the reservations of Morison and Pollard who felt that Isaac could have got a lot more out of his material. The book, after all, conformed to the stated purpose of the series and usefully reproduced samples of a great many types in excellent collotype. David Thomas's review in *The Library* was even more scathing than his earlier article.[22] Pollard was particularly irritated by his yapping about the high price of the books. Hanson's text on Government and the Press was published soon after Isaac's volume. It was commended by the critics for painstaking research in a difficult field.

As soon as the series was fairly launched Johnson was casting around for more titles. A letter to Pollard in April 1935 is full of ideas: 'PS [Percy Simpson] is so pleased with his great adventure [*Proof-reading*] that he vows, if he lives to finish Jonson, that he will go on to a large monograph on punctuation.[23] Why should we not include the symposium on spelling, of which you once spoke, in the series?' The evolution of spelling was taken up by Sir William Craigie, one of the editors of the *Oxford English Dictionary*, and George Watson who had worked with Craigie on the *Dictionary* and collaborated with him in the *Dictionary of American English*. But this time collaboration failed and Johnson had to report in January 1937: 'OBB History of Spelling. I am afraid this volume has fallen through for no other reason than because Craigie and Watson have fallen out'. Johnson himself did a lot of work towards a book on jobbing printing. At one time he invoked the aid of a young man who had greatly admired the first books in the series and had begged Johnson's help in getting a little of the same paper for his own private press. This was Vivian Ridler who later, of course, became Oxford Printer. The Oxford Books on Bibliography were not the only outlet for all this research. Johnson read a number of papers to the Double Crown Club and other bodies, including one on jobbing printing which was several times recast.[24] Strickland Gibson arranged exhibitions of printed material in the Bodleian from time to time and described them in the *Bodleian Library Record*.

The Cadell and Davies correspondence which Johnson had bought for a song in the dark days of 1932 was augmented by other Cadell and Davies letters which Johnson later found; and Besterman discovered more in libraries. After much editorial discussion about the best way to treat some of this extra material, the book was ready for publication in the summer of 1938. This time both the book and the series were warmly praised in *The Library*.[25] Johnson was commended for rescuing the Cadell and Davies archive and publishing it, thereby extending the scope of bibliography to include publishing and distributing history as well as that of printing, paper-making and binding. The reviewer was Michael Sadleir of Constable. As a bibliographer and a publisher with high standards of his own in book production, he was well able to assess both content and form of what he called 'this handsome series'. Johnson need not have worried that Sadleir might resent the competition to his own *Bibliographia* series.

For many years Johnson and Strickland Gibson had been working together on an edition of the first minute book of the delegates and also a history of the early years of the press which acquired the title *Print and Privilege at Oxford*. They had started on this even before the monographs were suggested. The transcript of the minute book had been ready for the printer early in 1932. But work was only intermittent; other things kept intervening. In 1937, for example, demands for special printing for the Coronation encroached on Johnson's spare time; but he and Gibson sometimes got together on a Sunday morning. Strickland Gibson must also have played a more important part in shaping the other volumes than is apparent from the surviving records, both in giving Johnson sensible advice, and perhaps restraining his impetuous enthusiasm, and also in supplying information to the authors. As Keeper of Printed Books in the Bodleian[26] and keeper of the University archives, he had an impressive range of knowledge and no one asked for his help in vain. He even remembered to send a postcard every spring to Chiang Yee, author of the 'Silent Traveller' books, when his magnolia tree was in flower so that Chiang Yee could come and look at it.[27] I suspect that much of the spade work for the first minute book and for *Print and Privilege* was done quietly by Gibson. The slightly flamboyant style of *Print and Privilege* may be Johnson's but the scholarly footnotes were Gibson's. Johnson provided the drive and enthusiasm but Gibson followed putting things in order. There is a revealing note from Gibson to Johnson saying: 'We really must survey all our material. It might be as well if I visited *you* at the Press tomorrow week (Sunday January 22) and reviewed the Corpus . . . All we want now is *Order*. Otherwise all is well.'

The war brought all this activity to a halt. Johnson took very seriously his responsibilities for organising fire-fighting in the vicinity of the Press, which included the Radcliffe Infirmary across the road, and he did not leave the Press day or night. Gibson was so depressed by the course of the war that in the summer of 1940 he burned all his correspondence and contemplated destroying all his bibliographical papers if the situation got worse. But in time things improved and in October 1942 Johnson wrote to Pollard: 'By one of the contrarities of war Gibson and I are trying to put the finishing touches to *Print and Privilege*. We meet again on occasional Sunday mornings and again we revive old memories'. The appendix of documents for *Print and Privilege* had been in type since the end of 1936, but the volume was not published until 1946, and then jointly by the Oxford Press as one of their *Books on Bibliography* and by the Oxford Bibliographical Society as their publication for 1941 and 1942. *The first minute book of the Delegates of the Oxford University Press, 1668–1756*, edited by Strickland Gibson and John Johnson, had been published in 1943, not by the Press, though they printed it, but by the Oxford Bibliographical Society. *Print and Privilege* was slow to achieve recognition. *The Times Literary Supplement* did not get around to reviewing it until the end of 1947, but then its reviewer described it as 'the most important contribution to the history of publishing which had appeared for many years' and 'economic history at its best'. He spoke of 'an original and exciting narrative' by 'two great servants of the present university'.[28]

Print and Privilege was the last title to be issued in the series, but was not quite the end of the story. In the mid-1960s the Oxford Reprint Series was launched. The Press wanted to reprint *Print and Privilege* (it was after all part of their own history) and after much searching of memories and records, its exact status vis-à-vis the Oxford Bibliographical Society was established and a facsimile reprint was issued in 1966. This time it was bound in the standard Oxford dark blue cloth. The Turner Berry and A.F. Johnson catalogue of type specimens was also on their reprint agenda; but here the Oxford Bibliographical Society had forestalled them and had arranged for a revision by James Mosely, Turner Berry's successor as Librarian at St Bride. It was published in 1984 as *British type specimens before 1831*.[29] Percy Simpson's *Proof-reading* appeared in the Oxford Reprint Series in 1970 with a new foreword by Harry Carter.

The later story of Morison's Fell Types which, in the course of its long history, featured briefly in John Johnson's programme, is well known. After Morison had finished with the *History of The Times*, Charles Batey, Johnson's successor as Printer, coaxed him into resuming work on it, and with the very considerable help of Harry Carter it was finished and printed by Batey's successor, Vivian Ridler, in as splendid a form as Johnson himself could have wished for.[30] In 1969 Pollard considered reviving the Chrestomathy and again, shortly before he died, he talked about it to Michael Turner and agreed that *Publishing History* would be a convenient forum for the publication of records of this kind. But of course he also used some of the material in other ways, notably in his Sandars lectures on *The English Market for Printed Books*[31] and in *Distribution of Books by Catalogue*.[32]

At an early stage in his plans for the series Johnson wrote to Milford: 'The truth is that I am anxious to make the monographs a foundation for something else in the future'. The 'something else' was to be a history of publishing in all its aspects. Pollard, who had suggested it, was asked to produce the usual synopsis. He called it 'Notes for a discussion of chapter headings for a possible History of Publishing in England'. It was in four parts covering the period from the introduction of printing into England until the defeat of perpetual copyright in the late 18th century, with an introductory survey of the commercial production and distribution of manuscripts.[33] In the succeeding 50 years a great deal of work has been done on many of the topics they reviewed and they would no doubt be delighted to know that there is again a possibility that all this will be brought together in a multi-volume history of the book trade in Britain.

References

1. This glimpse behind the scenes of the genesis of a short but influential bibliographical series is possible largely because the postal service in the 1930s was quick and efficient and the telephone had not yet superseded the letter as the normal means of contact. Johnson was in Oxford and Pollard in London and both filed carbon copies of outgoing letters as well as letters received. The largest collection is in the Bodleian Library (MSS Pollard and MSS Johnson); there are some among the archives of the Oxford University Press. I am grateful to the Library and to the Press for facilitating my study of them, and also to the Library of the Stationers' Company for preserving the dust wrappers of their copies of the books in this series. I owe particular thanks to Michael Turner for encouragement and advice and to Anthea Williams for letting me know of the letters at the University Press.

2. *Auctio Davisiana Oxonii habita*, a satire in Latin verse by George Smalridge, Bishop of Bristol, on the recently introduced technique of selling books by auction, was published in 1689 in the names of William Cooper and Edward Millington, London booksellers and the first book auctioneers in England. The Plautine scholar may have been Peter Thoresby Jones who produced an edition of Plautus in 1918.

3. 'Proof reading by English authors of the 16th and 17th centuries' in Oxford Bibliographical Society *Proceedings and Papers*, vol.2, part 1, 1928.

4. They are now in the John Johnson collection in the Bodleian, and have been catalogued by John Feather in *Book prospectuses before 1801 in the John Johnson Collection: a catalogue with microfiches*, Oxford Microform Publications Ltd for the Bodleian Library, 1976. Mr Feather has similarly catalogued the prospectuses in the Gough Collection in the Bodleian.

5. Letter from John Johnson to Stanley Morison, 10 February 1932.

6. Paper, i.e. the supply of paper, imported as well as home produced, for printing, was originally Morison's subject and was to include 'some thirty letters ready copied from the paper agents of the 17th century' [presumably from the archives of the Oxford Press]. Their negotiations about paper supplies were used by Johnson and Gibson in *Print and Privilege at Oxford*. The Bodleian library acquired about this time the paper stock ledger of William Bowyer, shortly to be published by the Bibliographical Society. Gibson, encouraged by Johnson, did a good deal of work on the paper monograph in the next few years.

7. Edwards of Halifax. The records are now in the Bodleian Library.

8. Printed in their *Publications*, 1947.

9. 'Booksellers' Bookbinding', unsigned article in *The Times Literary Supplement*, 10 March 1932 (no.1571) p.176; further notes by Pollard in the issue of 7 April 1932, p.256. The bookbinders' price lists were eventually printed in 'Some bookbinders' price lists of the seventeenth and eighteenth centuries' in *Economics of the British Booktrade 1605–1939*, eds. Robin Myers and Michael Harris, Chadwyck-Healey, Cambridge, 1985.

10. But he did not lose interest. *The Times and the Post Office* was published, by *The Times*, in 1946.

11. Johnson took a hand in this, and one weekend wrote a chapter which he passed to Simpson to incorporate.

12. It has been said of Chapman that he tended to attach less weight to content than to style while Johnson and Pollard were indefatigable researchers among original material. Milford would understand without being told that there was no way in which Johnson and Chapman could co-operate in this series. (Both Chapman and Milford were friends of T. J. Wise and supported him when *An Enquiry into the Nature of Certain Nineteenth Century Pamphlets* came out, but that embarrassment did not arise until two years later.)

13. People who knew Bersterman in his later years find it difficult to believe this picture of the young Besterman.

14. Graphically described in: Peter Sutcliffe, *The Oxford University Press, an informal history*, Oxford at the Clarendon Press, 1978, on which this account is based.

15. *TLS* 4 April 1935, pp.217–8.

16. *The Library*, 4th series, vol.xvi, no.3, Dec. 1935, pp.347–52.

17. *TLS* 22 August 1935, p.522.

18. *The Library*, 4th series, vol.xvii, no.1, June 1936, pp.111–6.

19. *The Library*, 4th series, vol.xvii, 1937, pp.230–4.

20. *Review of English Studies*, vol.xiii, 1937, pp.190–205.

21. *TLS* 9 November 1935, p.728.

22. *The Library*, 4th series, vol.xviii, no.2, Sept. 1937, pp.216–8.

23. Percy Simpson had already published one study – *Shakespearean Punctuation*, Clarendon Press Oxford, 1911.

24. Some drafts are in the John Johnson collection in the Bodleian Library (MSS Johnson *c*.29 and *c*.30).

25. *The Library*, 4th series, vol.xix, no.3, December 1938, pp.363–8.

26. The title Keeper of Printed Books did not come into use in the Bodleian until 1943 but Gibson had been in charge of the printed books as sub-librarian since 1931.

27. Chiang Yee, *The Silent Traveller in Oxford*, 2nd edition, Methuen, 1945, pp.159–61.

28. *TLS* 29 November 1947, p.617.

29. *British type specimens before 1831*. Oxford Bibliographical Society *Occasional Publication* no.14, 1984.

30. *John Fell, the University Press and the 'Fell' types* by Stanley Morison with the assistance of Harry Carter. Oxford at the Clarendon Press, 1967.

31. Sandars lectures in Cambridge, 1959, reprinted with an introduction by M.L. Turner in *Publishing History*, no.4, 1978.

32. *The distribution of books by catalogue from the invention of printing to* A.D.*1800, based on material in the Broxbourne Library*, Cambridge, 1965.

33. The general headings are:

    INTRODUCTORY. Before the introduction of printing.

    BOOK I 1476–1554. From the introduction of printing into England to the incorporation of the Stationers' Company.

    BOOK II 1554–1637. From the incorporation of the Stationers' Company to the Star Chamber Decree of 1637.

    BOOK III 1637–1695. From the Star Chamber Decree of 1637 to the lapsing of the Licensing Laws in 1695.

    BOOK IV 1695–1774. From the lapsing of the Licensing Acts to the defeat of perpetual copyright.

    The synopsis was apparently unfinished. In the only surviving copy (Bodleian Library, MS Pollard 275, ff.51–55) part IV consists of the general title only.

Proof-reading in the sixteenth, seventeenth and eighteenth centuries. by Percy Simpson.
First published 1935. Imp. 8vo, 264 pages, xvi plates, 4 facsimiles in the text. Price 45/-
Reprinted with a new foreword by Harry Carter, 1970 in Oxford Reprint Series.

Catalogue of specimens of printing types by English and Scottish printers and founders, 1665–1830. by
W. Turner Berry and A.F. Johnson. with an Introduction by Stanley Morison.
First published 1935. Imp. 8vo, liv, 98 pages, 24 collotypes. Price 42/-

The beginnings of systematic bibliography. by Theodore Besterman.
First published 1936. Imp. 8vo, xi, 81 pages, xii plates. Price 21/-
Second edition, revised, 1936
Troisième edition revue. Traduit de l'anglais, Paris 1950 8vo, 95 pages, xii plates

English printers' types of the sixteenth century. by Frank Isaac.
First published 1936. Imp. 8vo, xx, 60 pages, 80 plates. Price 25/-

Government and the press, 1695–1763. by Laurence Hanson.
First published 1936. Imp. 8vo, x, 150 pages, frontispiece. Price 21/-

The publishing firm of Cadell & Davies. Select correspondence and accounts, 1793–1836. Edited with
an introduction and notes by Theodore Besterman.
Facsimile reprint, 1967. First published 1938. Imp. 8vo, xxxv, 189 pages. Price 38/-

Print and Privilege at Oxford to the year 1700. by John Johnson and Strickland Gibson.
First published 1946. Imp. 8vo. viii, 212 pages. Price 42/-; also issued by the Oxford
Bibliographical Society with a cancel title as their Publication no.7.
Facsimile reprint, 1966 in Oxford Reprint Series.

WILLIAM TURNER BERRY (1888–1978) worked in the St Bride libraries from 1913 to 1958 except during 1914 to 1919 when he was in the RAMC. He succeeded R.A. Peddie as Librarian in 1922. He compiled, with H.E. Poole, *Annals of printing: a chronological encyclopaedia from the earliest times to 1950*. He wrote many articles on printing for the trade press.

DR THEODORE BESTERMAN (1904–76). His early career was in the Society for Psychical Research; he was also special lecturer in the London School of Librarianship from 1931 to 1938. In the next 15 years or so he was concerned with bibliographical sources, working for ASLIB on their *Journal of Documentation* and compiling his *World Bibliography of Bibliographies*. From 1952 he wrote mainly on Voltaire; he was director until 1973 of the Institut et Musée Voltaire which he founded.

STRICKLAND GIBSON (1877–1958) worked in the Bodleian Library, Oxford from 1895 to 1945, from 1931 as sub-librarian in charge of printed books and from 1943 as Keeper of Printed Books, a new title. He was Keeper of the University Archives from 1927 to 1945 and lectured on Bibliography. He founded the Oxford Bibliographical Society in 1922 and served as Honorary Secretary and general editor. He wrote a pioneer study of early Oxford bookbindings and edited the early statutes of the University. His other writings include a bibliography of Francis Kirkman and many bibliographical articles.

LAURENCE WILLIAM HANSON (1907–66) was an assistant keeper in the Department of Printed Books in the British Museum from 1931 to 1948, and Keeper of Printed Books in the Bodleian Library, Oxford, from then until his early death in 1966. His publications include 'English Newsbooks, 1620–41' in *The Library*, 1938, and *Contemporary printed sources for British and Irish Economic History, 1701–50*, Cambridge, 1964.

FRANCIS SWINTON ISAAC (died 1956) worked in the British Museum for about 10 years until 1939. He published a conspectus of all the types used in England and Scotland down to 1558, and he wrote a number of articles for *The Library*. He continued Proctor's Part II, *An index to the early printed books in the British Museum, 1501–1520*, and later produced the volume on the Italian and Swiss books.

ALFRED FORBES JOHNSON (1884–1972) of the British Museum published much on type design and calligraphy. He worked, while he was on the staff of the Department of Printed Books and after he retired, on the Museum's *Short title catalogues* of books printed before 1601 in France, Italy and the Netherlands and Belgium.

DR JOHN DE MONINS JOHNSON (1882–1956) was editing papyri and directing excavations for the Egyptian Exploration Fund from 1908 to 1914. He was Assistant Secretary to the Delegates of the University Press, Oxford, from 1915 until 1925 when he was appointed Printer. He built up an enormous collection of ephemeral printing which he gave to the University and continued to augment, classify and arrange it after his retirement in 1946.

SIR HUMPHREY SUMNER MILFORD (1877–1952) joined the University Press at Oxford in 1900 as assistant to the Secretary to the Delegates of the Clarendon Press. He was transferred to the London Office of the Press in 1906 and became Publisher to the University of Oxford in 1913. He retired in 1945.

DR STANLEY MORISON (1889–1967) was typographical adviser to the University Press, Cambridge, from 1923 to 1959 and to the Monotype Corporation from 1923 until his death. He was on the staff of *The Times* from 1930 to 1966. He edited the *Fleuron* from 1926 to 1930 and *The Times Literary Supplement* from 1945 to 1947. He published a great deal on type design, on the early calligraphers and on the history of newspapers. He edited the first four volumes of the *History of The Times*.

GRAHAM POLLARD (1903–76) was an antiquarian bookseller (in Birrell & Garnett Ltd) from 1924 to 1939. During and for some time after the war he became a civil servant, and returned to bibliography after an early retirement. His bibliographical interests embraced the commercial production and distribution of books from the 13th to the 19th centuries.

DR PERCY SIMPSON (1865–1962). After a period as a schoolmaster he became, in 1913, lecturer in English at Oxford and later Reader until 1934. His main study was the Elizabethan dramatists, Shakespeare, Marlowe and, above all, Ben Jonson.

Discussion following the paper

Contributors – Peter Stockham, Robin Myers, Michael Turner, Michael Harris, Keith Maslen, David Laker, Tony Lister, Giles Mandelbrote, Michael Turner, Don McKenzie.

It was after Graham Pollard's death, Esther Potter said, that his Sandars lectures were published from his surviving papers in *Publishing History* IV, and his work on bookbinding manuals was published by the Oxford Bibliographical Society in 1984. There was some further discussion concerning the relationship between the Oxford series and Michael Sadleir's (Constable) Bibliographia series; Esther Potter pointed out that the emphasis on original records of the Oxford books meant that there was no direct rivalry between the two projects. Someone commented that Laurence Hanson's *Government and the Press* did not fit easily into the framework of the series. Esther Potter answered that its inclusion was, in part, the result of John Johnson's identification of Hanson as: 'There is a man who performs.' There was some discussion on the profitability of the Oxford books and the high cost that there must have been, with both those and the Bibliographia series, for collotypes, good quality paper and so forth which would not have easily been recouped. Michael Turner observed that it was significant that those involved in the Oxford series were all working in the book trade. Discussion then turned on the group of individuals most closely involved, in particular Strickland Gibson. An enormous quantity of his correspondence has survived, with other people, widely dispersed. It includes a mass of postcards and small notes. Johnson and Gibson, like Johnson and Besterman, were very close friends who both had an otherwise restricted social life. Michael Turner remarked that Johnson thought that 'Gibby' had been very badly treated by the University.

Towards the end of the discussion talk turned to the relationship of the Oxford series to the general history of the book. Underlying the conception of the series was the sense that all the work was contributing to the construction of a national history, and in this it was well ahead of continental developments. The Bumpus exhibition of Oxford books in November 1930 gave an impetus to the Oxford Series. The originators, Pollard, Johnson and others were perfectionists and found it difficult to write on a limited subject because they had their eye on a wider horizon, that is to say, the history of the book trade as a whole.